Endorsements of the Shared Values Process®

PEPSI-COLA®

A Very Special Endorsement on a National Basis of the Shared Values Process®/Operating System. In 1989, the Pepsi-Cola® distributor (Alpac Corporation) on the West Coast of the United States instituted the Shared Values Process along with its advertising and public relations vendor Evans-Kraft. Four years later, in the early summer of 1993, needles were found in Diet Pepsi cans. The regional news story immediately became a national crisis when over 30 other cans from around the nation were thought to have needles. ALPAC responded immediately with the help of outside advertising and public relations groups, and partnered with the Food & Drug Administration to respond to the public's fears. Both Pepsi-Cola and Evans-Kraft used their Shared Values principles that had been taught to them by the Lebow Company to meet this crisis head-on. Here is what Pepsi-Cola stated in their brochure about the crisis, called: What Went Right!

The Pepsi 1993 Needle Hoax Crisis—"A crisis means accelerated events, unexpected turns and constant pressure. There is no time to think about what your company stands for. Those values have to be well entrenched. Ours were. By instinctually and constantly checking ourselves against what was best for our customers, we consistently made the right choices. Not just management, everyone. Our philosophy lighted our steps in the midst of the storm. Employees must be ready, willing and able to accept extraordinary new responsibilities at a moment's notice. The crisis quickly tests the relative strength of a guiding vision. Pepsi-Cola's vision statement embraces a straightforward philosophy:

> "We will be an outstanding company by
> exceeding customer expectations through
> empowered people, guided by Shared Values."

**(Taken from the brochure *What Went Right!*
produced after the 1993 Needle Hoax Crisis.)**

And the Shared Values they used in this crisis were 'Treat others with uncompromising truth,' and 'Put the interest of others before your own,' two of the eight Shared Values of the Heroic Environment®.

ENGEN Petroleum LTD. South Africa

"I am absolutely convinced that our decision to implement the Shared Values Process was a good one, and will benefit ENGEN OIL (Mobil Oil of South Africa) handsomely in the medium/long term."

Mpumellelo Tshume,
Director of Human Resources & Development,
Cape Town, South Africa,

(In the past the organization was named Mobil Oil, South Africa. ENGEN used the Shared Values Process to bring together their staff— a group of very diverse cultures that were not working well together. Their goal was to create "true transparency" amongst Africans, Native South Africans, and other ethnic groups. Please ask us for a copy of this independent report by a leading South African graduate business school on the results of the Process. Profits, morale, and brand increased dramatically. To receive the report: contactus@lebowco.com)

R.R. Donnelley & Sons Co.

"It strikes me that the principles of the Heroic Environment and Heroic Behavior are the kind of logical, common sense fundamentals of life that too often get lost in big business."

Roger D. Missimer,
Senior Vice President,
R.R. Donnelley & Sons Co.

Coca-Cola Enterprises

"The Concept of the Heroic Environment is the 'open marriage' of business and philosophy...it borders on organization without ego. Very simply, these eight principles say '...do what is right; treat others as you would expect to be treated...with trust and dignity.' It really deals with the essence of down-to-earth values."

Jim Stevens,
Chief Operating Officer,
Coca-Cola Enterprises,
Atlanta, Georgia

Author, Harvey Mackay

"In an easy read you can learn how to humanize your whole organization and turn everyone into a winner. I loved this powerful book. Buy it!"

Harvey Mackay,
Swim with the Sharks Without Being Eaten Alive

Think Federal Credit Union (formerly—IBM MID AMERICA Credit Union)

"I love the book. Your product line is rich. The applications far exceed my wildest previous imagination. This is a concept we are going to run with."

Paul Horgen,
President & CEO,
Think Federal Credit Union
(One of the most profitable Credit Unions in the United States!),
Rochester, Minnesota

Author, Kenneth Blanchard

"If you want your company to work, and people to care about each other and the good of the whole organization, read this wonderfully appealing book. Heroism in the workplace isn't fiction. It can come alive and make a real difference in our lives."

Kenneth Blanchard, Ph.D.,
Co-Author, *The One Minute Manager*

Author, Mary Boone

"Rarely is so much wisdom contained in such a compact, accessible package. People at all levels of an organization can benefit from the lessons of this book."

Mary Boone,
Author, *Leadership and the Computer*

John Sculley, Former CEO of Apple Computer

"Don't miss this book! You'll come away with some extraordinary insights into how great companies make the Shared Values Process an essential principle of their strategy."

**John Sculley, Principal,
Sculley Brothers,
and former CEO, Apple Computer**

Gabbert's Furniture

1996: "As I reflect upon where the organization is today in comparison to where it was before we started our journey together, there's not a moment's doubt in my mind that we chose the right path when we chose the Shared Values Process. The transformation has been remarkable, and I know the journey has just begun. For all you have done, and for all you will continue to do, I am eternally grateful."

And, now after 8 years!

2004: "Shared Values was introduced to our company in 1996. Today, in 2004, it continues to be a vital part of our corporate culture. It is not a fad. It is not the flavor of the month. Shared Values has staying power and the power to change an organization for the better, because it draws upon the basic truths of who we are as human beings and the kind of environment within which we desire to work. This is a simple book, filled with powerful truths."

**James (Jim) Gabbert, CEO,
Gabbert's Furniture,
Minneapolis, MN, Dallas and Ft. Worth, TX**
(An award-winning furniture retailer, nationally recognized for quality of service and excellence)

A JOURNEY
INTO
THE HEROIC
ENVIRONMENT

A JOURNEY INTO THE HEROIC ENVIRONMENT

NEWLY REVISED AND EXPANDED VERSION
THIRD EDITION

*A Personal Guide for Creating
Great Customer TransActions Using
Eight Universal Shared Values*

Rob Lebow

SelectBooks, Inc.

A Journey into the Heroic Environment: A Personal Guide for
Creating Great Customer TransActions Using Eight Universal
Shared Values
Copyright ©2004 by Rob Lebow

This edition published by SelectBooks, Inc. For information,
address SelectBooks, Inc., New York, New York.

Revised Edition
ISBN 1-59079-061-8

Library of Congress Cataloging-in-Publication Data

Lebow, Rob.

A journey into the heroic environment : a personal guide for cre-
ating great customer transactions using eight universal Shared
Values / by Rob Lebow.--Newly rev. and expanded version.
        p. cm.
Includes index.

ISBN 1-59079-061-8 (hardbound : alk. paper)

1. Job satisfaction. 2. Work environment. 3.Quality of work life.
4. Labor productivity. 5. Industrial management. I. Title.

HF5549.5.J63L43 2004

658.3'14--dc22

                    2004010469

Manufactured in the United States of America

            10 9 8 7 6 5 4 3 2 1

ACKNOWLEDGEMENTS

People come into your life in different and amazing ways. One of those people is a fellow who I am honored to call a 'good friend.' Randy Spitzer is a man who has from the very beginning been straight with me and our friendship. His integrity and honorable character have warmed me. His talents and creativity have added to my knowledge. And our co-authorship in *Accountability* (book two of the Journey books) has added to our appreciation of the other's gifts.

I want to recognize other important people who have contributed to this book. First, I want to thank Bill Gladstone, a one-in-a-million book agent, for his counsel, humor, and humility. These three character traits have comforted me over the past twenty years, and it is through his initial belief in the Journey book and me that my life has been changed forever.

I am honored to be an author at SelectBooks, New York. Kenzi Sugihara, my publisher, has talent, humor, and a strong vision and sense of purpose, and I look forward to future projects with him and his team. Todd Barmann, my editor, and Kenichi Sugihara, the art director for this book, have done everything in their power to support this project. And, thank you to Julie Schwartzman for the cover art and Kathleen Isaksen, our typesetter, whose quiet behind-the-scenes efforts are appreciated.

At the Lebow Company, there are many who need recognition for their inspiring efforts. Peter Dove stands out as a leader and major contributor to the Shared Values efforts over these many years. Additionally, our Lebow Company Associates and many of our clients and vendors have become friends because of Shared Values, for which I am grateful. Some have dedicated their lives and efforts to promoting Shared Values, and their support is meaningful and appreciated. Among those who have supported this dream are Donn Roberts, Jay Marshall, Robert Benson, Paul Horgen, Fred Green, Jim Gabbert, William Simon, Russ Dean, Barbara Nelson, Abdulrahman Tuwaijri, Dan Cook, Terry de Jonckheere, Henry Wallace, Bob Morse, Paul Demitriades, Jane Strickler, Jim Mahan, Pedro Aguirre, Gary Roden, Jerry Ask, Jan Ballard, Mike Bell, Roger Bennett, Carl Behnke, Bill Brokaw, Frank Cahill, Bob Chesney, Kevin Collette, John Mitzel, Dick Cross, John Eastham, Freidbert Gay, Steve Gerhardt, Jane Alberts, Phil Gerisilo, Tony Goedde, Bill Guinn, Bob Hamm, Dr. Ibrahim Mishari, Kathy Owen, Carroll Heyward, Chris Laszlo, Gary Lear, Denny McGurer, Bob Mitzel, Rich Meiss, Larry Nieman, Kathleen Norton, Emmanuel Okumu, Terry Emmerick, Alice Onduto, Maurice Orr, Roger Parker, Col. Mike Peck, U.S.A. Ret., Steven Piersanti, Tom Rausch, Dick Hultquist, Rick Samphoa, Don Dahl, Ken Shelton, Arynne Simon, Susan Silver, Michael Treadwell, David Tschanz, Alan Whitaker, Corey Williams, Richard Shutts, and Steve Pedersen. There are literally thousands more who love Shared Values, have touched our hearts, and have supported and joined our efforts on the Journey.

A huge thank you to Patti Pritchard, who heads up the Lebow Company office. She is a 'rock' of inspiration, calm, and a supreme professional.

And, a special thank you to my wife for her unflagging support, counsel, and love.

THANK YOU TO OUR CLIENTS
The Lebow Company—2004

Acura of Bellevue
Aguirre Inc.–Dallas, TX
Air Care
Alaska Airlines
Albuquerque TRANE
ALCA
American Banks Insurance Co.
American Home Assurance Co.
American International Co.
American Mail Envelope
AMS TRANE
Andover Printing
Anheuser Busch
ARCO Products
Armco Steel MEI International
AT&T Capital Corp.
Augat Corp.
Ault, Inc.–Minneapolis
Autodesk
Baltimore TRANE
Banta Prepress Groups
Bargreen Ellingson
Benson Honda, CA
Benson Kia, Petaluma, CA
Berg Inc.
Bestworth-Rommel, Inc.
Big Sur River Inn
BMW of Bellevue, WA
Boeing Commercial Aircraft
Boston TRANE
Boy Scouts of America, West Coast
Braas, Inc.
C&E Telephone
California State U., Long Beach
Cascade Auto
Cellular One, MN
Centennial Distributing
Centerline Piping
Central NY TRANE

Centrasota
Century Circuits
Champion Rentals
Charlotte TRANE
Charshaw (Stinker Stations)
Chicago TRANE
Children's Hospital, Seattle, WA
Christian Campers, IN
Cincinnati TRANE
City University, WA
City of Issaquah, WA
City of Richfield, MN
Coldwell Banker
Colonial Pacific Leasing
Color Response
Colorbrite
ColorMatrix
Columbia TRANE
Columbus TRANE
Computer Aid, Inc.
Connecticut TRANE
Crysteel Mfg.
DBI Architects
Dade Behring TAC
Damuth Services
Data Collection Systems
Dayton Rogers
Dayton TRANE
Denver TRANE
Department of the Treasury, U.S.
Detroit TRANE
Display Pack
Dow 680 Group
Dow Pharmaceutical
Eagan College
Eagle Distributing
Eaton Financial Corp.
Edmonton TRANE, Canada
Electrohome

Engen, South Africa
Engen, Zimbabwe
Environ. Conditioning Systems
Ernst & Young, Seattle, WA
Evans Kraft Advertising
Express Personnel
Excell Data
FairPoint Communications
Fargo TRANE
FirstContact, Inc.
Fisher Paper Box
FLEXcon
Flowers to Go
Ford Australia/NZ
Ford India
Ford Motor Co. HQ–Dearborn
Ford Philippines
Ford Thailand
Ford Thailand Associates
Four Seasons Cleaners
Fresno TRANE
Froehling, Anderson, Plowman & Wasmuth
Frontier F.A.S.T.
Frontier LDCS
Frontier Network Operations
Frontier Telephone
Ft. Meade, MD 704th Military Intelligence Brigade
Gabbert's Furnishings–Dallas, TX
Gabbert's Furnishings–Fort Worth, TX
Gabbert's Furnishings–Minneapolis, MN
Gatti Corporation
General Distributing
General Electric Capital Corp.
Georgia TRANE
GM Nameplate
Goddard Space Flight Center
Goodyear Tyre, Australia
Grand Rapids TRANE

Gray Line Tours
Greenville TRANE
Greenway Auto Mall
Group Health of WA, Bellevue Clinic, Renton Clinic
GTE Leasing Corp.
Group Marketing TRANE, La Crosse, WI
Guimarin, Inc.–South Carolina
HD Fowler
Henderson Homes
Halifax TRANE
Harper Mechanical
Hartford TRANE
Henry Lee/Smart Final
Hong Kong Bank
Honolulu TRANE
Horizon Air
HUD
Illingworth Corp.
Incstar
Indianapolis TRANE
Instrumentation Northwest
Interactive Ink, Inc.
Interlinq
ITRON Corp.
Jackson TRANE
Jacksonville TRANE
John L. Scott Real Estate, WA
Kansas TRANE
King Co. Credit Union, WA
Knoxville TRANE
LRC Electronics
LaCrosse TRANE Business Unit
LaCrosse Sales TRANE
Lakeview Village
Lane Energy Systems
Lease Insurance Corp.
Lexington TRANE Business Unit
Limbaugh Toyota
Little Rock TRANE
London, Ontario TRANE

Los Angeles TRANE
Lou Bachrodt Chevrolet
Louisville TRANE
Lower Umpqua Hospital
Lowry & Associates
Lozier Corporation
Lynchburg College, VA
Mankato College
McKenneys
Meade Group
Memphis TRANE
Miami TRANE
Michigan AirGas
MARCON Coatings
Minnetonka College, MN
Mitzel's American Kitchens
Modern Mechanical
Moly Corp., Canada
Monsen Engineering
Montreal TRANE
Moore BCS HQ
Moore BCS Logan
Moore BCS Mundelein
Moore BCS Thurmont
Moore BCS Windsor
Moore Research Center
Morgan Ohare
MTS NW
MTS Sound
NAELF Steel, MI
NCR
Nalco/Exxon
Namoi Cotton, Australia
Nashville TRANE
National Frozen Foods
New England Mechanical
New Orleans TRANE
Newport Telephone
Nissan of Fife, WA
North Jersey TRANE
Northeast Bank
Northwest Eye Center

Northwest Financial Leasing, Inc.
Nutron Nameplate
NY TRANE
Office of Executive Mgmt. (FEI)
Oklahoma City TRANE
Omaha TRANE
ORIX Credit Alliance, Inc.
Orlando TRANE
Orr Chevrolet
Orr Honda
Ottawa TRANE
Oxford Telecom
PACCAR Leasing
Paradigm Options, Canada
People's Mutual Telephone
Peoria TRANE
PEPI–Positive Employee Practicies
  Institute
Pepsi-Cola–Alpac West Coast Bottler
Phoenix TRANE
Piper Jaffray
Pitney-Bowes Credit Corp.
Port of Seattle
Portland, OR TRANE
PRISM/Microdisk Services Corp.
Provident Services
Prudential Insurance Corp., MN
Rasmussen College
Regina TRANE, Canada
Richmond UPG TRANE
RLD Associates
Roadrunner Transportation Co.
Roberts TRANE
Roemer Industries
Royal Truck Body
Rushville TRANE Business Unit
Russ Dean Ford, Pasco, WA
Rykoff–Sexton
S&W X-Ray
Sacramento TRANE
Salt Lake City TRANE
San Antonio TRANE

San Diego TRANE
Sanwa Leasing Corp.
Saturn of Fairfield, CA
Saturn of Vaccaville, CA
Saturn of Marin, CA
Saturn of Santa Rosa, CA
Saudi ARAMCO Information
  Technology
SEAFAIR, Seattle, WA
Seiberlich TRANE
ServCom Associates
Shade Allied Corp.
Siena Heights University
Sioux Falls TRANE
St. Cloud College, MN
St. Louis TRANE
State of Washington
Storer Equip. (Shreveport TRANE)
Subaru of Bellevue, WA
Tampa Bay TRANE
TCI West
Teklogix
TeleDirect International
Teltone
Texas TRANE
Think Federal Credit Union
Thunderbird Home Hardware
  Stores, Canada
Tokai Financial Services
Toledo TRANE
Toronto TRANE, Canada
Trabar Trucking
TRANE After Market Business Unit

TRANE BAS
TRANE Birmingham
TRANE Executive Group
TransOcean Products
Triangle Distributing
Uniglobe Travel
Universal Cooperative
U.S. Air Force Dept. of Defense
U.S. Foodservice–Las Vegas
U.S. Foodservice–LaMirada, CA
U.S. Foodservice–San Francisco
U.S. West New Vector Group
Valley Medical Center, WA
Vancouver TRANE, Canada
Vero Global/Risk Managed,
  Australia
Veterans Administration, U.S.
Viking Engineering
VIRACON
Vision Ease
Volkart May
Volkswagen of Bellevue, WA
W & H Pacific Engineering
Waco TRANE Business Unit
Walker Richer & Quinn
Washington Imaging Services
Westmark Hotels/Holland America
  Lines
Wichita TRANE
Wilkes-Barre TRANE
William Dierickx Corp.
Youngstown Univ. Facilities
Zetron

CONTENTS

Introduction: Twenty Years After The Journey Began   *1*

1 The Journey Begins   *7*

2 Defining the Heroic Environment   *17*

3 Walking Our Talk   *33*

4 The TransAction Zone   *51*

5 Understanding Heroic Behavior   *67*

6 The Four Corporate Personality Work Styles   *91*

7 Telling Someone You're Sorry   *109*

8 The Mystery of Organizational Success   *117*

9 The Curse of Conditional Thinking   *123*

10 The Role of the Navigator in a Heroic Environment   *133*

11 The Importance of Having a Tracking Motor   *147*

12 Restarting & Sustaining Your Tracking Motor   *153*

Epilogue: The Beginning of a New Journey   *169*

The Personal Work Style Assessment™   *173*

Index   *191*

Introduction

Twenty Years After the Journey Began

INTRODUCTION

Twenty Years After the Journey Began

It's been nearly twenty interesting years since a stranger wandered into my office and asked, "What do you *really* do here?" That stranger turned out to become, in his own right, a bestselling author and one of my great friends, but on that cold October afternoon in 1985, Roger Parker changed my life.

Frankly, before the question was asked, I thought I was performing the duties of a vice president of marketing for a Seattle software company, but the question stopped me dead in my tracks. That afternoon, after a bit of hemming and hawing, I told Roger that my true purpose was to help the organization create a workplace that would allow everyone to play at the top of their game. I was brought into the company to be the peacemaker between warring factions, at least that is what the board of directors hoped. But I really didn't have a handle on how to do that, nor did I expect that I would be successful. I had great confidence in my ability to bring a product to market, but I hadn't a clue on how to keep peace.

What I didn't realize that day was Roger would set me on a journey of discovery that has grown into an international training and consulting business on four continents—North America, Europe, Africa and the Middle East, and Australia.

Roger's question was truly disquieting. He literally challenged me to face myself, to address my purpose. For some reason, it hit a resonating chord that changed my life forever. That day, I set out on a new course that I have never regretted. Today the Lebow Company helps organizations make peace and, in the process, serve their customers at the highest standard possible.

A Journey into the Heroic Environment has changed hundreds of thousands of lives, just as Roger's question and interest touched mine. In this book, we unlock the secret to creating peace and fairness in any organization. The size of a company does not matter in the slightest. Industry, ethnicity, or religion do not matter. What matters is the knowledge that *we are all in the "People Business."*

The book has garnered many compliments and comments. It has been enlightening to see and hear all the ideas, reactions, and enthusiasm surrounding a journey I started alone two decades ago. Today, nearly 2,300 individual organizational sites have studied Heroic Behavior and the Lebow Company's teachings. Many have decided to embrace the simplicity of doing the right thing for others—a cornerstone of our guiding principles we simply refer to as *Shared Values.* The outcome of practicing Shared Values is that everyone wins. The customers win, teams and individuals win, the organization wins, and the community wins.

Shared Values has become a buzz word around the world; now we all need to practice these principles. Every week the press and media uncover yet another company, organization, or individual that has turned his or her back on the concepts inherent in Shared Values. Twenty years after the journey began, the 2002 Sarbanes-Oxley Act (a Congressional mandate) intensifies the need for ethics and values to become a front-and-center element within every organization, both public and private.

In 1985, we could not *give* this idea away. Frankly, many people felt that values were dead. I will leave that debate to you, the reader. Today we help organizations around the world create Shared Values workplaces. That is all I do every day. And I must tell you, I have never had more fun in my life.

In 1989, the idea of Shared Values became a *Process* that is protected by the United States Patent Office. Imagine…no one had ever taken the time to register Shared Values. Today, the Shared Values Process®/Operating System (SVP®/OS) has gained respect and interest from businesses and governments around the world, and the applications for Shared Values are multiplying.

In 1996, a Hollywood production group purchased the film rights. The film, *A Journey into the Heroic Environment,* premiered at a meeting of the American Society of Training and Development (ASTD) in Orlando, Florida, to enthusiastic audiences. As they say, if you enjoyed the book, you'll love the movie.

There are many new friends who have been attracted to Shared Values and the ideals of Heroic Behavior portrayed in this book. We are grateful for their commitment and friendship and wish them well on their journey. For those who have read the first or second editions of this book, you will note that we have salted this third version with new ideas and concepts. We continue to learn on a daily basis. We have also added more graphics. And as always, we look forward to your comments.

At the end of this new version, we have a short assessment instrument that you may want to take to identify the level of Heroic Behavior you personally exhibit in your organization. *The Personal Work Style Assessment*© tool is our gift to you. It is a shortened version of a larger index, developed by the Lebow Company, called the Values & Attitude Study© and is today the most definitive indexing device on Shared Values in the world—with over

2,300 benchmarked sites. If you would like your organization to take the Values & Attitude Study, email your request to contactus@lebowco.com. Background on the Values & Attitude Study has also been added at the end of this book.

Each day, we have the opportunity to create our Heroic Environment anew—I with my family, colleagues, and clients; and you with your family, organization, and customers. For nearly twenty years my daughter, Lauren, my wife, Sharon, and I have practiced acting Heroically as a family, something parents who read this book can understand in their own way and use effectively in their own lives. As a result, people have asked me to write a book on the family and to focus on Personal Heroics. I am encouraged by these requests and have assembled a series of guidelines based on the eight Heroic Behaviors that individuals, schools, and families can use. If you would like a complimentary copy of these family and personal guidelines, please email us at contactus@lebowco.com.

Sigmund Freud said, "True insanity is continuing to do what we have always done while expecting a different outcome." Shared Values now gives us the opportunity to do things differently and achieve more satisfying results with everyone. We wish you an interesting and fulfilling journey toward your Heroic Environment, and we know that with persistence and courage you will find what you are looking for. A special thanks goes to our clients and to you for your interest and support.

Rooting for Your Success!
Rob Lebow

Chapter One

The Journey Begins

ONE

The Journey Begins

Today would be a special day for John Spencer. He had just completed a job interview with a firm in Chicago, and it had gone well. The president of the company had taken the time to interview him personally, and John felt that this new company was trying hard to woo him away from his present organization. It was a good feeling, and he wanted to savor the moment for as long as he could. "Not bad, Spence," he reflected quietly with some pride.

The weather in Chicago is always unpredictable, especially in the winter. That morning, as he began his interview, the sky had been clear and the smell in the air crisp and fresh. Five hours later those pleasant conditions had dramatically changed. When John climbed into the cab, it was snowing hard and he knew that O'Hare Airport would be a zoo. By the time he arrived at his terminal, that heavy snow had turned into a blizzard and his flight had been canceled.

"Great!" John thought to himself, "Now what?" After a moment's indecision, John grabbed his phone and called Amtrak's 800 number.

On the fifth ring, an operator picked up. "Thanks for calling Amtrak; how may we help you?"

Thank God it wasn't one of those blasted automated voice systems. "Hi, do you have any sleeper compartments still available going to Denver today?" John asked.

"Yes, we do, sir and they're going fast. May I have your name?" John completed the reservation. Amtrak's *California Zephyr* would become John's home for the next sixteen hours.

He closed the phone, immediately opened it up again, and dialed his home number in Denver. "Hi, honey…Yeah, it went great. They loved me. I think they'll be offering me the job. Let's talk about it when I get home. Listen, my flight's canceled because of a blizzard, so I'll be taking the train home. I'll arrive in Denver at 9:38 A.M. tomorrow. I've got to run. I love you." John hung up with a self-satisfied grin.

The cab crawled through the blinding snow to the train terminal. In spite of the hassle, John felt a sense of guilty pleasure. He loved trains and secretly welcomed the time to unwind and think. He had a lot of sorting out to do.

From the responses he had received, John felt his interviews had been successful at this new company. Yet he was still unsure of what to do. Kathy was happy at her advertising job and was moving towards partner at the firm. This move to Chicago would end that possibility. Plus, she loved Denver and the three-year-old home they lived in.

John had another issue that was haunting him. His father had worked for the same company from the time he had left the Army until his retirement forty-three years later. Yet John, in the eight years since he had graduated from college, had already worked for two companies and was now considering moving to a third.

Somehow he didn't feel right about that. What about loyalty? Up until now, John had told himself that the other two companies had really left him. In each case, it was the company's fault. They had let him down.

John considered himself a successful and loyal employee, and his career at this production plant was a good one. The year before, he had been named assistant plant manager of the company's second-largest electronic components parts division, and with all the changes in the telecommunications industry, he believed his future was bright. But globalization had changed things dramatically. Most of his company's competitors had already moved their production facilities overseas and were building products just as good at half the price. John didn't know how long it would be before his firm made that same fateful decision, leaving him out in the cold. The company's executives said they would never relocate, but he and the other middle managers had their doubts.

He felt the company recognized him, but John felt frustrated and helpless about what was happening around him. A large part of his frustration came from the fact that he had been given a great deal of responsibility to carry out the existing policies without the ability to change or modify their impact on his people. Put simply, he was accountable for every little mistake he or his people made, but the responsibility for decisions was at corporate headquarters thousands of miles away. How could people in the Connecticut home office possibly know or appreciate the market conditions in Denver? How could they make decisions and policies that affected him and the other workers without even asking for input? And when they did ask, they didn't seem to listen. It seemed they'd already made up their minds. That's what angered him the most.

In the four-and-a-half years John had been at the plant, the Connecticut office had instituted program after program to "fix" the Denver plant. John knew that these "programs-of-the-month"—that's what the staff called them—didn't address the real issues that he faced every day. John was not a management genius by any means, but he knew these programs ignored the one element critical to making his operation work—*his people*. And the programs corporate headquarters implemented offended people. Ranking people, searching out faults to fix, measuring people's every activity was not the way to win friends on the assembly line or at the 30-by-60 inch desks.

So programs went in one year and out the next, and nothing changed. Maybe they used different words, but the outcome was always the same. The company's top-down approach to decision making had made implementing fresh ideas almost impossible. John was being asked to enforce policies that he knew were working against the organization's best interests. One Sunday, in a fit of desperation, John asked his father for some advice on the matter. His dad had said that he'd get his chance someday, but for now he should just keep his mouth shut and be a good soldier.

"A train trip will give me a chance to sort through this," John thought, as he weaved slowly down the narrow passageway in the rail car through the crush of travelers. Compartment 417-C was two car lengths away. Wet clothing gave off a pungent but not unpleasant odor. Besides suitcases, many passengers carried shopping bags filled with brightly wrapped Christmas gifts.

When he arrived at his semiprivate compartment, John's companion for the sixteen-hour journey was already comfortably seated next to the window, watching the people in the crowd. As John moved forward to lift his carry-on bag onto the overhead luggage rack, the stranger instinctively rose with his hand outstretched to support the bottom of the bag.

While taking off his overcoat and suit jacket, John glanced at his fellow passenger. He didn't understand why, but the stranger seemed to be someone with whom he immediately felt comfort-

able. There was a disarming air about the older man. John was surprised at himself—his typical response to a stranger was to be
standoffish and reserved.

As the younger man sat down, the older man extended his hand
to introduce himself. "Hi, I'm Stan Kiplinger, but everyone calls me
Kip." Kip's steel-blue eyes looked directly at John, revealing astute-
ness and a sense of curiosity lying just beyond their friendly twinkle.

As they shook hands, John introduced himself and added, "I
don't normally take the train, but it was a mess at O'Hare. Do you
travel by train often?"

Kip smiled and reflected aloud that when he started in business, there was little choice but to go by train. "You know, there's
something special about train travel which is missing in airplanes.
Trains are a great place to sort things out. Are you going home for
the holidays?"

John nodded. "My family and I have lived in Denver for the
past five years, and we really like it. Kathy, my wife, has a great job
that she loves and we have a really nice house and a two-year-old
who keeps us both plenty busy."

Kip nodded, thinking of his own grandchildren waiting for his
next visit. "Were you in Chicago on business? I hope you don't
mind my asking."

"I don't mind at all. I was here for a job interview." John
replied.

Kip nodded, knowingly. "I did my fair share of looking when
I was your age," he said.

"And did you ever find what you were looking for?" John
asked in a hopeful voice.

"No, I never did!" said Kip, amiably.

John felt the air go out of his throat. "Oh."

It was apparent to Kip that the small talk was over. He sensed
that he had been asked a serious question, one to which his
younger companion was seeking an answer. He paused a moment

before responding. "I never did find that perfect job, but I found something better."

The younger man's posture changed. John leaned forward, listening carefully.

"It took me a long time to realize that there was no such thing as the perfect job. All jobs have pluses and minuses. Instead, I learned that it's possible to find fulfillment and happiness in almost any job. In fact, I guarantee that you can, too!"

Although John tried not to show it, he was flabbergasted by the man's answer and could not command the words necessary to respond for some time. Here he was, agonizing over his career, possibly leaving his home, and asking his wife to sacrifice her job and move halfway across the country and this stranger was talking about job satisfaction as if it were within everyone's grasp!

John's skepticism overtook his politeness. "Just like that! You think I can find job satisfaction? I don't even know what I'm looking for!" John realized that his bottled up frustration had just made an unscheduled appearance—and he regretted it.

The older man smiled almost enthusiastically. "I understand your frustration and skepticism. After all, that's a universal problem—what to look for."

At that moment, the train lurched forward, briefly interrupting their conversation. John, mesmerized by the sense of increasing speed, stared out the window while Kip's outlandish guarantee played over and over in his mind. John wondered how Kip could be so enthusiastic and confident. Everything in the younger man's mind blurred in a series of flashes: his family's reluctance to leave Denver, his most recent interview in Chicago, his father's loyalty to *his* company, and finally, his hunger to experience a work situation that would give meaning and purpose to his life. As his mind churned with these thoughts, his uncertainty grew along with his discomfort.

The silence was broken by Kip's words. "I hope you enjoy the train ride. Most people find the motion and sound soothing."

Kip's voice brought John back to the present. Without reply-
ing, John abruptly asked, "Mr. Kiplinger?...Kip, were you *serious*
about what you said?"

"You mean about guaranteeing that you can be happy and ful-
filled in your job?" Kip chuckled. "When I was your age, I was just
as frustrated and skeptical as you."

"What changed?"

"I was lucky. During my early years, I came across several people who helped shape my thinking and outlook. One of those
people was a man I met on a train ride. Come to think of it, not
unlike this one. His name was Dan Turner, and he was a sales
manager from Rochester, Minnesota. I was explaining to him
what was wrong with my job, why my fellow workers and I were
unhappy, why it was management's fault, and why I deserved better. I rambled on about looking for the perfect job. Dan listened
for a while and then asked me point blank, 'So, what are you doing
to improve the work environment at your company?'

"I was stopped in my tracks by his question. What did that
have to do with me? I couldn't affect the work environment. I just
carried out the policies. I didn't have the authority or power to
change anything! The work environment wasn't my responsibility.
That was management's job. Then Dan said to me, 'Stop looking
for the perfect job. Instead, help your company create a better
work environment.'"

John broke in. "What did he mean by that?"

"John, Dan believed that the secret to job satisfaction is the
way you treat others and how it causes others to treat you. Over
the years, your job-related tasks change, but the environment you
work in becomes more important to finding fulfillment in your
work life. Dan went on to suggest that the essence of this idea
centers on the values we share with others.

"Over the years, I've met other people who have reinforced
this sense that our Shared Values about our work holds the key to

our greatest job satisfaction. I believe this is the right way of thinking about job satisfaction. It is entirely dependent on a work environment which is created by individuals within the organization who agree to agree on what certain values mean to them personally—their *Shared Values,* as we call them now."

John was almost disappointed in what he heard. He had always felt that job satisfaction was related to other things. He had never considered the work environment as a factor in achieving job satisfaction, nor had he ever considered Shared Values as a factor in his job satisfaction. He thought all business environments were pretty much the same and that values were best left at home.

"Kip, I'm not sure I agree. I don't get it. My job isn't exciting anymore. What does that have to do with the work environment? From my experience, job satisfaction is tied to things like duties, title, and power, not to mention salary. Business is business. I don't really see a place for values at work. At home, yes, but at work…well, I'm just not sure."

At that moment, a sharp knock on the door broke the flow of conversation. A porter in a starched white serving jacket stuck his head in the door and asked if they were going to want an afternoon snack. Kip turned to John and said, "Their pies are great; would you care to join me?"

John nodded. At that, the older man rose to his feet in anticipation, and they both started the long walk back to the dining car.

On the way to their table, John realized that his concept of job satisfaction and Kip's could not be further apart.

Chapter Two

Defining the Heroic Environment

TWO

Defining the Heroic Environment

O nce they were seated at a table in the dining car, the waiter handed a menu to each of them. Kip turned to John and said, "Where were we?"

John put down the menu. As respectfully as he could, but still with an edge to his voice, John said, "You were telling me that my job satisfaction is tied to the Shared Values in my work environment, and I wasn't buying it. I don't find my job satisfying anymore. I feel I'm not allowed to be creative or to do those things I believe are the right things to do. What does this have to do with a better work environment or the values I share with my coworkers?"

"Look, John," Kip said, "in the beginning, all jobs are exciting, just like a new marriage. But typically, the thrill wears off and the atmosphere becomes more political—more charged with hidden issues, resentments, fears, and the like. People begin to worry more about protecting their position in the organization than about excelling. And if someone else comes up with an idea, they feel threatened.

"Imagine you come up with an idea at work. Are the folks at corporate happy about it? Probably not, and here's why. If you come up with a great idea, there's a fellow at headquarters who feels self-conscious because he didn't come up with the idea first. Now let's reverse it. If someone in corporate has a sensational idea, is the field happy? Probably not! The field figures that corporate folks don't really know the business environment or the field's customers well enough, so the idea is viewed with suspicion."

John nodded in agreement. "Yup, that sounds like my company."

Kip smiled. "The sad part is that everyone loses when this happens. The employees lose because of a lack of trust, and ultimately, the customer's experience is diminished. It seems that many people have their own agendas. They blame others for mistakes instead of taking responsibility, and they only do those things that make them look good in the eyes of management. Jack Welch of General Electric suggested that if we're facing our boss—because we want to please him or her—then our backs are to our customers."

John could see the older man's passion and let him continue without interruption. "But contrary to what you might think, most people don't want to be small-minded. They want to make a difference. I don't know anyone who, as they get out of bed in the morning, turns to his or her significant other and says, 'I can hardly wait to fail at work today!' No, I believe that what they want is to contribute to something bigger than their own self-interest—to be of benefit to others. It's just that most work environments, instead of fostering unselfish behavior, discourage this very vital drive in people. I believe that people want to be great. We all want a place in the sun, and most of us want to share the satisfactions of success with those whom we care most about.

"Imagine what would happen in a work environment if people were given the freedom to act the way they really wanted to act—with courage, creativity, and independence from fear of criticism, or worse. And when people are respected and appreciated, they want to contribute even more, to rise to their true potential. I call that kind of place—a place where people act heroically—a *Heroic Environment.*"

"A Heroic Environment, what's that?" said John.

"A Heroic Environment is a place that nurtures those who work there. Playing at the top of your game becomes the standard in a Heroic Environment. You can't imagine how happy people would be in such a place."

"Oh, yes, I can," said John. "But do places like that exist? Or is that just your idea of work heaven?"

"Yes, of course they do," laughed Kip. "True, they are all too rare, but they do exist. And wherever they exist, regardless of the industry, great things happen for the employees, the company, their customers, and the community."

"But how can I find such an environment?" John persisted. "Or better yet, how can someone like me help create such an environment?"

Kip could hardly suppress his pleasure at knowing that his younger companion understood what he was suggesting. He now knew that his instincts about John's leadership and character qualities were not misplaced. "John, the list of organizations practicing Shared Values is growing every day. But here's some additional good news. When you go back to work, you can create a Heroic Environment starting tomorrow. But before we plunge into this any further, let's order."

For the moment, John had completely forgotten that he was in the dining car. The conversation had unexpectedly captured him with all the possibilities it offered.

As Kip ordered his hot chocolate and John his coffee, John glanced out the window. The blizzard had turned the fields of the Illinois countryside into a picturesque land of snow. A white carpet stretched as far as the eye could see, interrupted only by the flash of telephone poles whisking by. John could feel a new optimism swelling in his chest, but he was not quite ready to let go of all his doubts and fears.

"John," Kip said, breaking the silence, "to answer your question about creating a Heroic Environment, let me first tell you where the name originates. In ancient Greece, heroes were those who acted unselfishly, who put the interests of others before their own. I'm convinced that such nobility is an integral part of most human beings around the world. People will rise to meet their challenges when treated with respect, trust, and dignity.

"But to create a Heroic Environment, all individuals in the organization must agree to follow certain fundamental principles. There are only eight of them, but they are all critical. *If even one of these principles is missing, you don't have a truly Heroic Environment.*"

Kip fell silent for a moment. He realized that he was about to share in a few hours with John what had taken him a lifetime to learn. He could only hope that the younger man would appreciate his offering.

"John, are you sure you want to hear all this?"

"Kip, you have no idea how much!"

Reassured, Kip found an extra paper napkin and started jotting down:

The Eight Principles of the Heroic Environment®

1. **Treat others with uncompromising truth.**
2. **Lavish trust on your associates.**
3. **Be willing to mentor, and be open to mentoring from anyone.**
4. **Be receptive to new ideas, regardless of their origin.**
5. **Take personal risks for the organization's sake.**
6. **Give credit where it's due.**
7. **Be honest and ethical in all matters.**
8. **Put the interests of others before your own.**

John turned the napkin so he could read it more easily. It seemed a long while before he looked up. "You know, Kip, what you've written here is not new, but I've never worked in a place that actually practices this philosophy. Oh, sure, everyone uses the right words. But there's usually such a gap between the words and the deeds that no one takes them seriously. To really put these principles to work—that *would* be something!"

"Good, John," Kip answered. "You understand how important it would be to implement and use these principles and yet how difficult the operational issues would be. So let's get into some detail so you'll know that these principles and the practice of introducing them into any operation is tough work—but it is more than possible."

Kip began. "The first principle of the Heroic Environment is *treat others with uncompromising truth*. John, what do you think that means?"

"I guess it means that everyone is told the truth all the time— that whether the news is good or bad, all the team members are informed about what's going on instead of being left in the dark or, worse, deceived."

Kip nodded. "Really, there is no other practical and sensible way to treat people. After all, if there's bad news, people find out anyway. Keeping the truth from teammates or management only causes anger and mistrust in the long run. On the other hand, telling the unvarnished truth early on brings the members of the team closer together and creates supporters instead of bystanders. And, when everyone on the team is involved in solving the problem, the chances for success increase."

"I wish my company's top management practiced this principle," replied John. "We always hear bad news through the grapevine."

Kip nodded and continued. "The second principle is *lavish trust on your associates*. Notice that I'm not just saying 'trust people.' I'm talking about trusting them and making them *feel* trusted. Do you remember the very first time someone you respected showed you how much he or she trusted you?"

John thought for a second. His eyes brightened with the recollection. "It was my dad. He had just brought home his new Oldsmobile. I was sixteen and had only recently gotten my driver's license. Dad handed me the keys and said, "Why don't you take her for a spin, son?"

"How did it feel?" asked Kip.

"On the one hand, great. I felt so grown-up. But on the other hand, I knew I would rather die than disappoint him. No teenager has ever driven a car more carefully."

"That's *exactly* what I'm talking about," Kip said, with enthusiasm. "When people *feel* trusted, they'll do almost anything under the sun not to disappoint the person who gave them the gift of trust. But if we put all kinds of strings around our trust, the reverse happens. People feel helpless and, ultimately, angered by this treatment and this literally undermines teamwork."

John nodded with perfect understanding.

"Now let's talk about the third principle, a rather interesting one—*be willing to mentor, and be open to mentoring from anyone.* Let me tell you…"

"Well, this one I know something about," John interrupted. "I had a mentor in my first job. He was my boss.

"He was unhappy with my disorganized writing style—he couldn't understand my memos and reports. So he set aside several hours to help me, and then kept monitoring and evaluating my writing. He kept doing this with me for several months until I became quite a good writer."

Kip smiled. "Good, you do understand something about mentoring. But there is much more to it. Let's take a look at the origins of the word. It's a Greek word that comes from Mentor, the loyal friend of and adviser to Odysseus. You see, mentoring goes beyond teaching someone a skill. True mentoring involves teaching, advising, and befriending. Under this definition, do you currently have a mentor? And more importantly, are you *yourself* mentoring anyone else?"

John shook his head no.

Kip continued. "In a Heroic Environment, everyone is responsible for mentoring others."

John was puzzled. "Wait a minute. What do you mean everyone is responsible for mentoring? I thought only *managers* should act as mentors to their subordinates."

"In most organizations, that's the way it is. But in a Heroic Environment, people mentor unselfishly because they understand that their success depends on the success of everyone on the team.

"Here's an example. Let's say you're leading a convoy of ships during wartime, and the ships must stick together for maximum mutual protection. Most of your ships can travel at eighteen knots per hour, but two ships can travel at only ten knots. How fast would your convoy travel?"

"That's easy," said John. "Ten knots."

"Right. Even though you've got ships that can go much faster, you're required to slow them down to keep in formation."

"I get it," said John. "Organizations aren't much different, are they? If you have people who are lagging behind in knowledge, understanding, or commitment, the whole organization slows down. The faster you can get everyone up to speed, the faster the business progresses. Right?"

Kip nodded.

"Yes, each day, there are literally hundreds of ways coworkers can help each other gain more information and understanding. In the Heroic Environment, everyone is a mentor because everyone has something to contribute. Employees also mentor their managers without fear of any negative consequences. Heroic bosses know they have much to learn from their staff and welcome their input, and one telltale sign for managers that their staff are afraid of them is that no one ever mentors them."

"Okay, I understand," said John, looking down at the napkin. "Isn't this next value, *be receptive to new ideas, regardless of their origin,* related to the previous principle?"

"Yes. In a Heroic Environment, ideas can spring from all corners—even from the newest or most junior employee. In fact, everyone learns to listen to new ideas regardless of their origin because no one has a monopoly on good ideas. They may come from fellow workers, vendors, consultants, articles, books, and most importantly, customers. It's hard to believe, but in our fast-changing world, there are still many organizations that act as if the only good ideas come from the home office. Not only does that approach shut out good ideas, it also puts too much pressure on leadership."

"I know exactly what you're talking about," John said, bitterly. John's tone had a hard edge. "Three months ago I sent a detailed proposal to my company's home office. It took me weeks of extra work at home to prepare. You know what? They didn't even bother to reply."

Kip nodded. "And how did that make you feel?"

"Rotten. In fact, that might have been the last straw that made me decide to look for another job. One thing's for sure, I won't go out of my way for them again!"

"That's the perfect example of what I mean. When an organization is not receptive to new ideas, they are losing potentially vital information. Just as important, they're demoralizing their most talented, creative workers. And when ideas are no longer proposed, the organization becomes brittle and vulnerable to market forces. It's an organizational version of hardening of the arteries."

"The next principle really baffles me," said John. "What do you mean by *take personal risks for the organization's sake?*"

"Have you ever heard people say, 'play it safe; why take a risk?' This is the attitude you find in lots of organizations, and it's the kiss of death. Risk-taking is one of the most vital activities an organization must engage in if it is to survive and thrive. An organization must encourage its members to put themselves on the line by allowing them to express their ideas without fear of ridicule, or worse.

"This concept is important for two reasons. First, individuals need to be challenged for their own personal growth; and second, an organization unwilling to look at problems from fresh perspectives is an organization unable to respond to change." Kip paused to make sure the younger man was following him in this important discussion before he continued.

"Recently I read an interesting story. It went something like this. A group of researchers wanted to study cultural taboos. As I understand it, they placed five chimpanzees in a comfortable primate habitat. In one corner of the habitat, they placed a nine-foot ladder leading up to a platform. On the platform, they placed a large bunch of ripe bananas.

"Of course, as soon as the chimps discovered them, one of them moved to the ladder and began climbing upward towards the bananas. Immediately, this chimpanzee was knocked to the floor of the habitat with a powerful blast of water from a fire hose hidden under the platform. Next, the other four chimps were doused with a powerful blast of cold water. After the chimpanzees recovered, one of the chimps cautiously approached the platform, only to be knocked off the ladder by another blast from the fire nozzle. Again, another blast to the rest of the group followed. After the second dousing, no one from the group would go anywhere near the ladder.

"Next, the researchers replaced one of the animals in the habitat. This chimpanzee, new to the group and unfamiliar with what had previously occurred, soon approached the ladder leading to the bananas and was immediately attacked by the other four more experienced chimps. In an instant, they literally dragged this unsuspecting innocent away from the ladder.

"One by one, each of the four remaining original chimpanzees was replaced by a chimp new to the habitat. Of course, each newly introduced chimpanzee would soon become curious about the bananas and would eagerly approach the ladder. And, each time, the other chimps in the enclosure would aggressively attack the new chimp to discourage him from going near the ladder.

"The researchers continued to replace each chimpanzee in the enclosure until a third generation had been introduced to the habitat. Despite the fact that not one of the original chimpanzees who had been doused by the fire hose remained, each new chimp continued to be attacked by the rest of the group when they wandered anywhere near the ladder."

Kip concluded his example with sadness in his voice. "Each successive generation of chimpanzees had learned from the previous generation to avoid the ladder or risk being attacked by the group. And because the attacking behavior continued despite the fact that none of the original chimps remained, the researchers concluded that  culture and traditional thinking, the taboo of avoiding the ladder, had been established in the habitat."

John knew all too well what Kip was talking about. Soon after he had started his first job, he saw the career of a bright manager ruined because he championed an idea that was out of favor with his immediate bosses. The frustrating thing was that the very same idea enabled the company's leading competitor to substantially increase its market share. He also remembered the time a new employee commented on how his former company would have solved a problem. His reward was an icy stare from his supervisor and the response, "Well, that's not how we do it around here." Still, John had a question. "Suppose someone has an original idea, the organization implements it, and it fails?"

Kip nodded in understanding. *"Of course* it's important that the organization makes every effort to implement ideas that work. But on an appropriate basis, it's essential that people be allowed to fail when they take the risk of staking a claim. Obviously, the more talented people will make more right decisions and should be rewarded accordingly. In a Heroic Environment, people should not be attacked for failure. After all, if the organization approves the idea, it belongs to everyone."

"Isn't the next principle the other side of the coin, *give credit where it's due?"*

"In a way, you're right. Many organizations don't give people a sense that they're appreciated. On the other hand, other organizations give praise so indiscriminately that it loses its meaning.

Employees want to be treated like adults, not children. More than anything, they want to feel there is a rationale for praise and promotions. They want to *understand* the rewards given and *feel* that the reward and praise system is fair."

John understood all too well. "It seems as though half the promotions given by my company are questioned by the staff. Sometimes the resentments are so strong you wonder how the plant functions at all. You'd think people would be glad to see fellow employees being rewarded."

"In a Heroic Environment, the staff understands the reason for a promotion," said Kip. "While they may or may not agree with it, they don't question the innate fairness behind the reward, so they aren't resentful. In fact, in a fully functioning Heroic Environment, people are genuinely happy for a peer's success."

"Kip, I'm really curious about the next principle, *be honest and ethical in all matters.* I think I know what this means, but please explain."

"Most of us think of ourselves as honest people. Yet I recently read a survey that concluded over 80 percent of U.S. workers believe senior managers are to some degree dishonest. And unfortunately, the media are eating up the weekly scandals on Wall Street. Obviously, there's a perception among employees that their leadership is not operating with full integrity, which means that employees can also rationalize not acting with total honesty themselves. The problems this thinking causes are horrendous, ranging from internal theft to the leaking of vital information to a competitor. And the final result of a disregard for integrity is the disintegration of the organization's morale and self-respect.

"A company with a Heroic Environment in place insists that all its business transactions are reviewed for their ethics—not just whether the transaction is legal, but also if it's the right thing to do. Here's a three-part test that's as simple as can be.

Three Part Test

1 · *Is it good for the Customer?*
2 · *Is it good for the Organization?*
3 · *Is it good for the Community?*

It's not easy in today's world to say yes to all three. But remember, I didn't say this was easy. I remember a time when people would not take unfair advantage of an opponent. Today, that's not always the case. Yet of all the principles in a Heroic Environment, none is more essential."

John could see some long-buried pain in Kip's eyes when he talked about the issue of integrity, but he didn't probe further. He pointed to the last principle, *put the interests of others before your own self-interests,* and said, "This sounds too good to be true."

"I won't apologize for that," said Kip, smiling. "But it is really true that when people focus their efforts on what's good for the organization as a whole, rather than on their own narrow interests, everything and everyone thrives." At that point, Kip stopped talking.

John sat silently for what seemed to him an eternity. Finally, he let out a low whistle. "Trying to employ all of these principles is some task, isn't it?"

"I suppose it is, John," Kip said seriously, focusing a hard stare at the younger man. "But then, with all due respect to those who search for quick fixes, developing and nurturing a Heroic Environment is far too important to be trivial. What is needed are people willing to commit themselves to the creation and sustenance of a Heroic Environment where they work. You'd be amazed at what would happen to our country's revitalization if more and more organizations were run this way. Just look at failing organizations and countries. There's always a reason for their lack of success, and often the problem lies with their values. John, I'll leave it there for the moment."

"Kip," John's voice filled with emotion, "I can promise you that I will not forget what I'm learning here."

Kip felt a rush of paternal affection toward the younger man. "Well, Pilgrim," he said with the best John Wayne imitation he could muster, "I reckon there's even more for you to learn on this here cattle run."

Both burst out laughing, mostly in relief that the emotion-laden moment had passed. Walking out of the now-empty dining car, they headed back to their compartment.

Chapter Three

Walking Our Talk

THREE

Walking Our Talk

When they reached 417-C, John excused himself to stretch. The train ride reminded him of the long rail trip he once took with his parents to visit his mother's relatives. Gradually it all came back: the friendly people he'd met, the adventure of train travel, and the exhilaration he'd felt walking to and fro on the rhythmically rocking train.

He stopped to stand between two cars to feel the clatter of the train wheels and their dislodging gyrations. A surge of raw energy went through him as the curtain of time lifted momentarily. He now remembered that it was on that train trip that he had first kissed a girl. For a moment, he was fifteen again.

The magical moment passed as quickly as it had come, and his mind returned to the present. As he reviewed his extraordinary encounter with Kip, he was struck by how close he had come to settling into a mediocre career without ever finding the secret to job satisfaction. Although he had done well by most standards, he was in a rut and he knew it in his heart. He wanted his life to have meaning and purpose. Instead, for the past few years, he had been coasting, and he was just beginning to admit the truth to himself.

Also, he felt keenly the strong competitive winds from overseas. And with his company's faltering grasp on a decreasing market share, he knew firsthand that his country's manufacturing industry was in trouble. If he could only do something to bring new respect to the term "Made in America," *that* would be something worth working for!

John's mind drifted back to his most recent job interview. Sure, he'd enjoyed the warm reception he'd received. But there was something all too familiar about this new company. He now clearly saw that their management style was not fundamentally different from the one he was thinking of leaving. Yet somehow, it didn't make so much difference now. He was on a journey of discovery and he felt a new power. By using the concepts of the Heroic Environment emerging in his conversation with Kip, maybe his career could have meaning and purpose beyond his own self-interest. And maybe he could become the leader he had always dreamed of becoming, rather than the victim he currently felt himself to be.

John hurried back to his compartment, drawn by the power of Kip's ideas. He knew that he only had a few hours to master the principles that could change his life, and he didn't want to waste a moment.

As he entered the compartment, he saw Kip sitting with his eyes closed, his head resting against the window glass. Kip opened his eyes, smiled, and straightened himself up, but he remained silent.

"Kip, I have a lot of questions. Can you help me understand how to use Shared Values to create a Heroic Environment?"

Kip thought for a moment. "Many organizations have plaques on their walls proclaiming great values: 'We believe in people,' 'People first,' 'Quality is our first job,' 'We are committed to innovation,' and the like. Well, don't believe these slogans until you talk to their people.

"In the old days, we'd call this *walking the talk,*' and what it means is that the people who write lofty slogans should live by them. Unfortunately, that's not always the case."

"I know what you mean," said John. "When I was in school, I remember my track coach used to ride us constantly about staying in training, but the coach smoked like a chimney! After that, it was hard to trust him."

"That's exactly my point," responded Kip. "Many organizations think that by putting up slogans something magical will happen. But the only thing that really changes behavior is when their proclaimed values are practiced at every level, including at the top of the organization. Then, and only then, will values move down through an organization. Shared Values need to be lived, practiced, communicated, and discussed daily.

"John, if we live our lives in silence, there's a pretty good chance that we'll send the wrong message to others. So, if we've established a set of Shared Values that we subscribe to, we need to establish a language that has meaning and purpose." The older man paused.

After a time, Kip went on. "Always remember—what we allow, we teach!

"You know, the ideas surrounding Shared Values are so important that I'm never sure where to begin. You might think of them as 'internal advertising.' After all, most businesses spend one heck of a lot of their operating budget on external advertising to attract and retain customers, but spend only pennies on their own people. And when organizations do invest in training often it's centered on 'fixing employees'—an approach that never works. John, a company's employees are its most important customers and its best advertisement. And remember, employees should never be placed in the wrong to make the external customer right. Ninety percent of the time, it is the terribly inflexible systems, processes, and rules that are at fault and not our staff members.

"Let's go back to the issue of consistently 'walking our talk.' Setting standards around our Shared Values is the key. And that means not only talking about telling the truth, but also establishing guidelines around each one of our values."

John broke in. "So, if I understand you correctly, the way you ensure that your Shared Values are consistently practiced is to establish the standards for each of your values. Boy, that seems like a tough job."

"John, I'm afraid that there are no shortcuts to establishing Shared Values, either within an organization or between two people. If you want the benefits, you need to first invest the time necessary. Most organizations that practice Shared Values have invested *years* in the process. That's because the journey of Shared Values never ends, just as a truly meaningful relationship is never static. Issues will arise that will cause us to focus on addressing a particular element of our agreements; with Shared Values, we now have a roadmap to follow."

"Now, this is an important point as well." As Kip spoke, he wrote on a piece of paper to underscore his remarks. "Think of it this way. Most organizations go for the quick fix. They don't mean to, and they believe they're doing what's right. They introduce a program to fix this or that in the hope it will stick. Instead of focusing on the deliverable to the customer, they focus on the structure or system and start counting the output and measuring the people instead of studying *the flow of the work* and *addressing all the variables* that customers demand and expect from them.

Most of the programs control-based organizations focus on are in one of three major categories: *incentives* to motivate, *performance-based systems* to measure output, or *structural redesigns* to streamline an operation's redundancies and thereby reduce overhead. But these programs lack the 'people' side and rarely benefit the customer. And when one of these programs does identify or address the contribution of people, it falls short of delivering on the one element that is needed—trusting people to be both accountable and responsible for making the transaction work for the customer. You see, trusting people is the foundation for any change we want to make. And this change is really a change in our belief structures."

John interrupted Kip. "'Program of the month' is what we call them," he said.

"And how do they work?" asked Kip, already knowing the answer to his question.

"They aren't doing what we hoped they'd do, but they keep on coming," said John, as they both smiled. "First, we had *Management by Objectives,* which turned into managers filling in the numbers. Then they threw *Quality Circles* at us, followed by *Total Quality Management.* We no more finished *ISO/QS 9000,* and they stuffed *Balanced Scorecard* and *Stack Rankings* down our throats. And now they're priming us for *Customer Relationship Management!* We've been benchmarking other organizations for the past few years, observing how other operations are employing *Process Engineering,* and we'll be introducing something the Connecticut organization calls *Core Competencies* pretty soon."

John's mood turned more serious. "You know, even though each one of these programs seemed important to us when it began, our enthusiasm for it always trailed off. And, even when we tried to keep it going with heavy incentives, threats, or worse, it never lasted. It's as if something was still missing in all our efforts to change the way we do business."

Kip nodded knowingly. "Yes, there is something missing, John. Remember, I used the word '*Process*'. Well, I used that word for a very special reason. Organizations with the best intentions introduce programs to support their people and their systems, unknowingly undermining, in many cases, the simple truth of every organization, regardless of size.

"In a rush to improve productivity and profits, or to stay competitive in the marketplace, they ignore their greatest asset—the inherent wisdom and goodness of their people. Instead of putting in place a set of Shared Values that has a universal resonance—one in which trusting people is the foundation of the belief system to make the transaction successful—they focus on short-term programs to solve their immediate problems and challenges. Almost all the programs you mentioned are both worthwhile and appropriate under the right circumstances, but they'll never *stick* until everyone feels respected, safe, listened to, and valued. Also, it is imperative that the programs selected are selected by the Front-Line Workers and not by management. So to provide a foundation for anything you want to accomplish, first implement Shared Values, *then* introduce the applications that make sense to your business. But let the workers decide which tools to use and when. That makes the most sense." Kip paused, then continued on to another subject.

"When I was growing up, my dad used to talk to me about the difference between **Sunday Values** and **Everyday Values.** He'd say, 'Kip, your Sunday values are important only if you intend to wear them for the other six days of the week. If not, keep your mouth shut. At least that way they won't call you a hypocrite...or worse!'"

"That's pretty straight talk," said John.

"Yes, it is, and it still applies today."

"I've also heard this called *espoused values* versus *actual values*," replied John, thoughtfully, "but frankly, it never made much of an impression on me before now."

Kip nodded. "Over the years, I've seen a lot of angry, disillusioned, betrayed people who never recovered their trust once they saw what was behind their management's Sunday Values. Preaching without integrity is explosive stuff and needs to be handled carefully. Believe me, if you say one thing and do another, you'll eventually be found out. Great care needs to be taken in both the style and content of our actions and communications. We need to pay conscious attention to what we say and how we say it.

"*Words without actions and actions without words can't successfully create or sustain a Heroic Environment.* Leaders from the frontline to the boardroom need to embrace a philosophy of ethics and integrity in everything they do, from the most basic transaction to the most important decision. John, nothing goes unnoticed in an organization.

"The best way to check out a new company is to look at how they walk their talk. If a company's Sunday Values and Everyday Values aren't aligned, or in balance, go elsewhere."

John decided to make his next question more personal. "Okay, I understand," said John. "But how do I, from a position with very little power, put the concept of walking the talk into practice organization-wide?"

"Good, you obviously understand that change doesn't start with top management, but with you! I'd like to have a dollar for every person who complains that management won't change. Well, the fact that management won't change isn't the problem. The problem is, are we, as individuals, ready and willing to change?

"Nevertheless, your first job is to start sharing these ideas with your top management as well as with your fellow employees. You see, there are two types of values that every organization needs in order to succeed—*Business Values* and *People Values*. These two sets of values define an organization and provide the foundation for unlocking and discovering its Heroic Environment.

"I've come to recognize that *Business* and *People Values* are in a dynamic tension with each other. Think of them not as a core set of values, like most business schools teach, but as a scale that needs to

ORGANIZATION-WIDE VALUES

PEOPLE VALUES

BUSINESS VALUES

be in balance and which is always in motion and sensitive to the slightest change in pressure. The customers and employees never see values as anything other than how the organization and its representatives behave every day, especially when the organization or its people don't think anyone is watching. That's why I say that the scale is both sensitive and dynamic.

"John, the greatest mistake I ever made in managing my company in the early years was to think that there was only one set of core values and that no one standing on the outside of my operation would see my inconsistencies.

"I came to learn the truth the hard way about core values—*they didn't exist*. What existed were the organization's everyday values. Yes, our behavior was seen and felt by everyone, our employees and our customers!

"I always felt that people were important, and how people were to be treated was one set of our organization's values. But the funny thing was that every time a business decision was in conflict with how we wanted to treat our people, we decided in favor of the business—and was that a big mistake! We seemed to always pay for that neglect in increased turnover, dissident behavior, lack of productivity, and decreased employee loyalty.

"It wasn't until years later that I realized that the reason we turned our back on our people wasn't because we didn't believe in what we were saying, but because we didn't understand how to achieve a balance between our Business and People Values and where our values were actually placed in our business. John, the truth is that everyone sees your values—and as much as you'd like to hide them or spin them, you can't.

"Unlike what our business experts and consultants have been teaching for decades, our values were not in the core of our operation." Kip drew what he believed would show John what he was suggesting, where tactics were the filtering device for all actions and decisions, and *not an organization's values.* This model, Kip had come to see, was tragically flawed.

"Note that our filtering device is the tactics we use or the spin we put on everything we do in this type of organization. No, John, values weren't at the center of our operation as we thought, and the idea of spinning the truth was easy in this design. But at the very outer limits of our business—for all to see and judge us on every day—were our tactics…at least that is what we thought. And, boy, were we wrong!

The "Concentric" Model of a Tactically Driven Organization

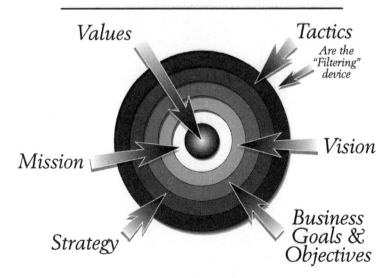

Values

Tactics
Are the "Filtering" device

Mission

Vision

Strategy

Business Goals & Objectives

"The funny part was that we were a lot more transparent to our employees and customers than we thought. And this meant that the concentric depiction and interpretation of a core set of values was all wet.

"Once we started using the Eight Heroic Principles of Shared Values and the standards surrounding each principle, we were able to successfully manage both sets of values—Business and People Values—and reach nearly every goal we wanted to achieve."

Kip then sketched his interpretation. It showed a sphere that exuded Shared Values and touched every part of all the other elements of an organization.

Kip went on with another important insight. "During the early times, our employees challenged us on everything we did, especially since they were accustomed to us spinning every announcement and decision we made. We had become, in the eyes of our staff and customers, *the boy who had cried wolf too many times,* and we were paying dearly for these past transgressions.

The "Molecular" Model of a Values-Driven Organization

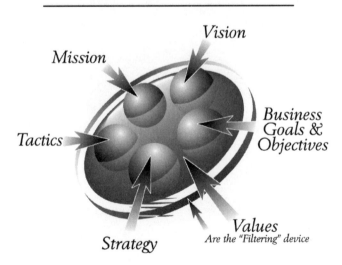

"At first it was exhausting, until our people and customers began to see a consistency in our actions and decisions."

At that, Kip took some paper from his briefcase and started to draw the first of several charts relating to Business and People Values. By this time, John was recognizing the importance of Kip's words and had decided not to interrupt him for the time being with any questions.

OUR BUSINESS VALUES
(Business Values must possess the emotional power to be personalized)

Business Values	Individual or Group Performance	Organizational Performance
Use your best judgment ... to meet the unique needs of each customer at the TransAction Point	1 2 3 4 5	1 2 3 4 5
Take responsibility... for removing TransAction Blocks. Challenge the way we do everything and find a way to improve it	1 2 3 4 5	1 2 3 4 5
Be accountable... for delivering Great Customer TransActions	1 2 3 4 5	1 2 3 4 5
Use Shared Values... in every transAction	1 2 3 4 5	1 2 3 4 5

"Here's a rough example of a set of Business Values," Kip continued.

"Business Values are those things which an organization must do every day to be successful. Now, I'm not suggesting that you should incorporate any of these into your operations, but only see them as good examples."

Kip continued. "A company's beliefs and actions concerning quality, customer service, community involvement, and business practices are good examples of what I mean. For the most part, Business Values are directed toward how we relate to creating great customer transactions. If a Business Value is not directed to either an internal or external customer transaction, then we probably are missing the mark.

"You will also note that we don't normally list profits or goals in our Business Values. When I bring this up, it causes controversy in certain circles of the business community. So let me explain the context of my comments about profits. Believe me, I like profits just as much as the next guy...but with a big 'but'!

"Over the past thirty years I've personally done a 180-degree turnaround concerning profits and have come to believe that profits are the outcome—not the goal—of our Business Values. Let me give you some examples to make my point.

"Imagine a doctor who is in it for the money. Imagine a teacher who only focuses on the kids' National Achievement Scores. Imagine a pharmaceutical operation or food processing plant that is only concerned with making a profit.

"If profit becomes the goal, I believe there is a great risk that we will miss the entire point regarding why we're in business or what our purpose is in life. Money should be the public expression of the success of our work. Profits should come from giving service and value. Business success for some is a 'win-lose equation,' but this equation is always temporary. No, profits are not a successful expression of Business Values nor should they be listed.

"They are, in my opinion, the measure or outcome of our transactions; and further, I believe that every staff member must understand how their efforts support the Business Values of their organization—that their individual efforts must be translated into individual purposes for getting up in the morning. And it is from this personalized drive to succeed that a *Keen Internal Vision* is created. Not until a vision is imbedded in our people, by their choice, can we achieve sterling profits and stellar customer transactions.

"John, you will know that you've arrived as a leader when your staff describes their purpose as being part of a team to get to the moon safely, or to leave no child behind in our education system, or part of the team to cure cancer. Now that may seem overly dramatic to you, but you will meet someone later tonight at our stop in Denver who believes she is part of a team that will change the American railroad industry.

"Of course, if you talk to twenty different companies, you'll get twenty different sets of Business Values, but typically there are similarities between companies.

"A simple exercise is to look at the list of universal Business Values, then grade yourself and your organization on how well your performance matches your values on a daily basis. You can use a scale of one to five and see how you and your company stack up.

"Don't forget that we are constructing a balance, so the counterbalance is our **People Values**." Kip took another piece of blank paper and drew the next chart. "People Values indicate how the company believes staff members and customers should be treated."

"It all starts with our People Values. So in a way, they are even more important than our Business Values. Remember, it's your people who support and carry out your Business Values and who you count on to make great customer transactions. If the people inside your organization don't feel that they're part of a supportive environment, a Heroic Environment, they won't take care of your Business Values, *the values that your customers transparently see and*

PEOPLE VALUES

(People Values are how we treat each other and our customers.)

People Values	Individual or Group Performance					Organizational Performance				
Telling people the truth	1	2	3	4	5	1	2	3	4	5
Trusting people	1	2	3	4	5	1	2	3	4	5
Mentoring people	1	2	3	4	5	1	2	3	4	5
Being receptive to new ideas	1	2	3	4	5	1	2	3	4	5
Taking personal risks	1	2	3	4	5	1	2	3	4	5
Giving credit	1	2	3	4	5	1	2	3	4	5
Honesty	1	2	3	4	5	1	2	3	4	5
Interests of others	1	2	3	4	5	1	2	3	4	5

viscerally experience every day."

John could see that the older man was no stranger to people and to organizational evaluations. John noticed immediately that the Eight Heroic Principles were Kip's People Values.

"John, in filling this out, use the same process as in the Business Values chart. Between the two of these, you'll be amazed at how clearly you can diagnose your organization's strengths and weaknesses when it comes to Shared Values. And this is the key to all performance, both on a personal and on an organizational level.

"I've seen evidence over the years that the practice of Shared Values is linked directly to profits. No single element will forecast the success of an operation quicker than measuring its level of Shared Values. And there is even a work environment study that does this effortlessly for you. This organizational tool is used around the world to identify these issues, and you might want to get your hands on it sometime.

"Remember, if there is a wide gap between your Sunday Values and your Everyday Values, you aren't walking the talk, and the combination of this misalignment and the resultant employee cynicism will eat you alive."

John knew that he was settling in for some interesting conversation before they reached Denver, and he sat back to enjoy the fun of it all.

Chapter Four

The TransAction Zone

FOUR

The TransAction Zone

Kip's voice brought John back to the conversation.

"Let me give you an example of how this applies…" Kip continued, not realizing that John was a thousand miles away and was just returning to this conversation. "As you know, most customers don't ever meet all the people who support a retail clerk. So in a way, you could say that the clerk is just the tip of the whole organization's iceberg. And this pretty much applies to just about every department and organization, from grocery stores to schools, hospitals, printing companies, technology businesses—I could go on and on.

The TransAction Point

"Front-Line Workers come into contact with customers at what I call the TransAction Point. Within every transaction, we face a *moment of truth*. If we deliver a great customer transaction, our customers will likely reward us with repeat business. This is true whether your customer is found internally or externally. Treat every transaction as a gift to your customer, and you'll never be sorry."

"That's a wonderful idea, thinking of a customer transaction as a gift."

"When you treat every interaction with a customer as a gift, the transaction is driven by the customer's needs, not by the organization's processes, rules or policies. And this is a huge idea. To make this happen, you've got to trust people on the frontlines to make the transaction *without supervision.*"

"O.K., so let's say I buy what you're saying for the moment." John asked, "What happens to management? What's their role in all this? And what happens when something goes wrong with the customer transaction?"

"When that happens, folks on the frontline get together and find a way to fix it. Management's role is to encourage people on the frontlines to explore new ideas and to experiment. They don't step in to fix problems or to criticize. Everyone is focused on the breakdown of the workflow. So together they roll up their sleeves and study the cause. And almost every time it's a system error that blocks the transaction.

"Very rarely is it a people issue. No one is focused on the blame game. If a difficult conversation with an individual is needed, it is performed within 24 hours between peers who are counting on the person to support the transaction. Management's role is to create a safe, constructive learning environment where everyone can be partners in 'working the work!'

"John, at this point we really need to make some sense of all of this. You see, if we remain in the role of the traditional supervisor, we can never enjoy the benefits of the TransAction Zone. So, to pull off TransAction Zone performance, I first need to introduce you to a new role for the old supervisor I call the new **Wise Counsel**. John, this role is important for both supervisors and managers." Kip pulled a chart from his briefcase and showed it to John.

THE FIVE WISE COUNSEL ROLES AND HOW THEY AFFECT FRONTLINE WORKERS TO BECOME SELF-DIRECTED PARTNERS IN THE CUSTOMER CENTRIX TRANSACTION

Wise Counsel Role	Growth Pain	A Partner Emerges
Coach	*Helps others learn and grow regardless of their role*	*Student*
Counsel	*Helps others discover their own answers without imposing answers or judgments*	*Problem-Solver*
Resource Connector	*Connects staff with financial support, manpower, time and other resources needed to deliver* Great Customer TransActions	*Resource Seeker*
TransAction Steward	*Helps Front-Line Workers understand that it is their responsibility to identify and remove TransAction blocks to improve the operation's Transactions*	*TransAction Point Owner*
Visionary Leader	*Helps everyone understand how their work supports the organization's purpose and helping each individual create their own* Keen Internal Vision	*Self-Directed Worker*

"This idea of creating self-directed Front-Line Workers is crucial if we want to achieve great customer transActions. John, please note that these five roles are the pathway to creating great TransAction Zones and true partnerships between Wise Counsels and Front-Line Workers."

"Kip, this all sounds too theoretical to me. Could you give me a real-life example?"

"Sure I can. Let me tell you about the world famous manufacturer, Toyota. They have four important lessons for us all. Their approach is a perfect example of how to create TransAction Zone thinking and Wise Counsel behaviors, even though they never use this terminology." Kip picked up a pen and wrote and began to explain his four points:

Lessons from TOYOTA:

1. **There is no substitute for direct observation.**

   "Toyota recognizes that relying solely on reports, surveys, narratives, data, and statistics to know what is happening is not an effective way to stay in tempo with their business. This 'direct observation' approach is in direct contrast to how we in America manage. In the West, we often rely solely on data and reports and seem not to want to patiently observe the workflow."

2. **Proposed changes should always be structured as experiments.**

   "In America, we're inclined to make a 'big deal' of change and want to make major leaps in innovation to show our boss that we're impacting the bottom-line. Often these traumatic changes create problems for management, labor, and customers. But for Toyota, change is defined as 'five-second improvements,' something almost any organization can handle with ease."

3. Workers and managers should experiment as frequently as possible.

"In Japan's Toyota plants, workers average 50 changes every two and a half shifts, which is about one change every 22 minutes! Just the idea of that many changes would give most American managers a nosebleed. When I introduce these statistics, many Americans discount my example as an exaggeration, not believing that it could possibly be true. It's beyond their imaginations!"

4. Managers should coach and not fix problems.

"Managers shouldn't assume responsibility for removing TransAction blocks. Removing TransAction blocks is the responsibility of the workers! Again, this runs completely contrary to the role supervisors and managers play in America because in America, fixing problems is management's job! In contrast, Toyota's most senior operational managers position themselves as teachers and coaches, not technological specialists."

After Kip finished speaking, John read over the list of four lessons from Toyota and reviewed the chart of The Five Wise Counsel Roles, then looked up and said, "Well, this explains a lot. Recently, I was at a manufacturing and service conference where one of the speakers talked about the contrast between Ford and Toyota. Here is what he said, and at the time I thought he was exaggerating. First, he said that Toyota was financially worth more than Ford, General Motors and Chrysler-Mercedes all put together. That was pretty hard to believe, but it was what he said next that threw me completely. The second point that he made was that it took Ford about nine months to make a change to their production line, while it only took Toyota three and one-half hours!"

Realizing that John understood completely the points he had been making, Kip said, "John, let me summarize what I just said so you can use this in the future." He spoke as he wrote.

SEVEN KEY IDEAS FOR MAKING THE TRANSACTION ZONE WORK

1. Management's role is to not take control of or responsibility for the mistake.

2. Management encourages Front-Line Workers to explore new ideas and to experiment with new approaches.

3. Management is no longer in the blame game.

4. Management and Front-Line Workers are focused on the workflow. They jointly identify TransAction blocks that inhibit Great Customer TransActions.

5. Management creates a safe and constructive learning environment where experimentation is encouraged.

6. Management views Front-Line Workers as partners in 'making the work work.'

7. If a difficult conversation needs to occur with any individual, management supports the conversation between the peers, but does not take ownership of the solution."

John shook his head. "That's certainly *not* the way we handle problems at our plant. I'll bet I spend at least twenty to thirty percent of my time fixing these kinds of problems or running interference, so one of my folks doesn't go up against the *hangman*. That's what they call the general manager behind his back, and he's really just a nice guy with a lousy role to play."

"I know, John. Early in my career I was the hangman in my company, and I hated it! So this is all good news for top management and for supervision as well. No longer is there a hangman role for anyone. And that is because in a Heroic Environment, management understands that solving problems from the top-down is just too slow these days. People on the frontlines need to be able to make the transaction *immediately*, and not fear that they will face the hangman.

The Pyramid

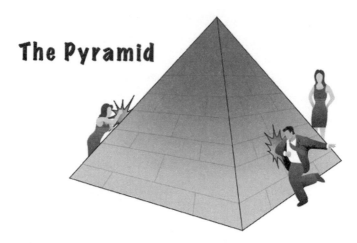

The Product, Price & Process Drive the Transaction

"By the way, I spell transAction with a capital 'A' in the middle of the word so that the emphasis is on immediate Action. You might think of the people on the frontlines as the organization's real CEOs. They are entrusted to make the decisions for the customer just like a CEO does in an old, slow, top-down 'Pyramid' environment."

"I never thought of it that way, that the Front-Line Worker is the CEO," agreed John. "But that's so true. I'd say I judge an organization by how I'm treated by the first people I meet—and if I'm not treated well, I won't go back."

"We're all like that. Yet, most organizations don't seem to understand that. Like I said before, to the outside world front-line people are the organization! Take a look at the training and education budgets for most organizations and you'll see that almost all the dollars go to teach supervisors how to take control instead of how to give up control." Kip paused to let this soak in and then continued in a less serious tone.

"John, there is a story I want to tell you that I think will punctuate what we've been discussing. Several years ago, United Press

International reported a human interest story that caught my eye. And after I read it, I didn't know whether to laugh or cry.

"Here is how it goes. In Spokane, Washington, a plainly dressed, older man caused quite a stir. This man was in the process of paying his parking fee when the attendant informed him that he could get his parking stub validated inside the bank where he'd just done some business at the bank's ATM machine. By doing this he could save two dollars.

"Feeling that two dollars saved was two dollars earned, the man returned to the bank to get his parking stub stamped. After patiently waiting in line for several minutes, he approached the next available teller and requested that his parking stub be validated. The bank clerk asked what transaction had been processed as she suspiciously eyed the poorly dressed older man. For some reason, the bank teller was not in a generous frame of mind and refused to validate his ticket. Well, the old fellow became upset and started to raise his voice.

"A supervisor was attracted to the activity and listened to his teller's comments. Earlier that week, the supervisor had been to a company training seminar on supervising and team building and thought he knew just what to do and how his decision would support the rules of the bank."

"I guess he stepped in and validated the man's parking stub," said John.

"Well, that's what he wished he'd done in hindsight. But instead, he followed what he had learned in his supervision classes about following the rules. He supported his clerk's decision and refused to validate the man's parking stub.

"Here was their reasoning: The transaction that the man had performed was a bank withdrawal on the outside of the bank at their ATM machine and, therefore, it was not considered a 'complete bank transaction.'

"Well, the man was furious and asked if a withdrawal inside the bank was a transaction worthy of the two-dollar parking validation. The supervisor said that it was. So the man withdrew his life savings from the bank, got his parking stub validated, walked across the street, and deposited a little over $2 million in a competing bank!"

John's mouth opened wide in amazement.

Kip continued, "Here's the lesson to be learned. When we don't have our Business and People Values universally understood and in balance, we're often influenced by control-based training programs and company policies and processes that may be well-meaning in a general sense, but don't serve our customers and employees. When organizations let products, prices or processes drive their transactions, situations like this happen every day. Most are not reported in the national news, but they happen. When you add the extra ingredients of judging people by their appearance and treating them as outsiders, you've created a volatile recipe for failure.

"The bank, by not understanding the value of working with customers and letting them drive the TransActions, lost a valued account. Had the older man been someone the teller knew, or if he hadn't been shabbily dressed, perhaps the outcome would have been different. But special circumstances should not be necessary for customers to be treated with respect. The problem is, in most top-down Pyramid organizations, employees are hostages to the policies and customers are outsiders. And both the employees and the customers are victims who can't do anything about it."

"I wonder if this bank is still treating customers this way?" pondered John.

Kip just shrugged, then he said, "How many customers do we chase away who go silently into the night without a fuss? Yes, we all take cues from others. You know what role models are. Well, the treatment of people is a learned behavior, and one that's perpetuated through role models within all organizations.

"If the people we work for and with treat us with respect, then we in turn continue this behavior toward others. That's why organizations have personalities of their own. In a Heroic Environment, every employee is taught to respect others and to create Great Customer TransActions with all customers, regardless of who they might be or might turn out to be."

"I get it, Kip," interrupted John. "They don't have to be taught to respect others because in a Heroic Environment, they learn that from the way they're treated."

"John, let me show you how a well-known national retailer, Nordstrom, takes care of this challenge. These folks have been successfully selling merchandise for nearly 100 years. Today they have over 100 retail stores. Each does well over $100 million per year and they employ over 50,000 people. Take a look at their employee handbook. Look at how they handle the issue of trusting their Front-Line Workers to make the transAction."

Kip pulled out the Nordstrom Employee Handbook, a roughly 5" X 7" laminated card. "Look at what it says: 'Welcome to Nordstrom. We're glad to have you with our company. Our number one goal is to provide **outstanding customer service**. Set both your personal and professional goals high. We have great confidence in your ability to achieve them.

"'Nordstrom Rules: Rule #1 **Use your good judgment in all situations.** There will be no additional rules. Please feel free to ask your department manager, store manager, or division general manager any question at any time.'"

WELCOME TO
NORDSTROM

We're glad to have you with
our Company.

Our number one goal is to provide
outstanding customer service.

Set both your personal and
professional goals high.
We have great confidence in your
ability to achieve them.

Nordstrom Rules:

Rule #1: **Use your good
judgment in all situations.**

There will be no additional rules.

Please feel free to ask
your department manager,
store manager or division general
manager any question
at any time.

nordstrom

John looked at Kip's 5" x 7" card in amazement. "Wow... unbelievable!"

Kip sat silently by John and he let the implications sink in. Then he broke the silence, saying, "A lot of well-meaning organizations put together customer service programs, customer relationship management courses and quality-assurance systems. But very few empower Front-Line Workers, sales persons, manufacturing workers, teachers, or governmental workers to call the shots to satisfy the customer like Nordstrom. They hire people they can trust and then trust them completely."

"But don't you need some controls in place to be successful?"

"John, it seems to me that it would be a lot cheaper and more effective if companies *really* understood how simple solving their problems actually is. You cannot produce lasting results unless you first have the proper environment in place and understand that the Business Values and People Values that we discussed earlier are two separate sets of values. People Values are not a subset of an organization's Business Values, but a legitimate partner in a dynamic equilibrium.

"When both these sets of values are in balance, you have a Heroic Environment. But when either your Business or People Values are top-heavy, one emphasized to the neglect of the other, your work environment will go out of balance and the dynamic equilibrium that you need to create great customer transActions will be destabilized or worse, destroyed."

John seemed to grasp the significance of Kip's explanation, but had one more question.

"Kip, why do you call this balance of the two sets of values a dynamic equilibrium?"

"Because it's never stabilized or fixed, John. Over the course of time, new priorities and situations arise that destabilize our values and challenge our beliefs, policies, and strategies. Let's say, for example, that something happens at your plant in Denver that affects the way you do business: A competitor from overseas introduces a product in direct competition to your bread-and-butter moneymaker and they undercut your price by thirty percent. What your organization does in response, both internally and externally, will communicate more about your organization's *actual values* than any words, slogans, or plaques ever could."

"That would be tough to manage if it happened to us," said John.

Kip smiled and said, "John, it's not a matter of *if*, it's a matter of *when*. What you do about it when it happens will define whether you have a sustainable Heroic Environment or not. The organizational structure of a Pyramid approach is incredibly dangerous over time. You see, there is not only a large Pyramid that our external customers see but consider the implications that the internal customers encounter—all our supervision and Front-Line Workers. They don't encounter one Pyramid, they encounter numerous Pyramids—everything from finance, to manufacturing, to engineering, to help-desk, to IT. Each Pyramid is an *empire* with its own set of rules, traditions and do-not-enter signs!"

The Internal Structure

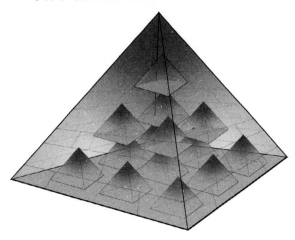

At that, Kip drew multiple Pyramids inside the larger Pyramid that the external customers see. John just shook his head. "I know exactly what you're saying!"

Kip continued with some caution in his voice. "Heroic Environments are easy to create in good times. The real challenge to our fundamental principles and Shared Values comes when times get tough. That's when the Pyramid becomes the coconspirator of the competition. It works against the organization's speed, agility, creativity, purpose and integrity. And it undermines the transActions just when you need a free hand to maneuver with. The true character of individuals and organizations is best tested during challenging and competitive times."

John began to understand the greater significance of the Heroic Environment and the importance of creating a balance between the two sets of values—Business Values and People Values. This was no pie-in-the-sky dream for creating fulfilling working conditions, but rather a foundational idea, a road map for the overall success of any organization.

Kip looked at his pocket watch after realizing that it had long since turned dark outside their window. "Well," he said, "why don't we get something to eat before we talk ourselves right past dinner?"

Chapter Five

Understanding Heroic Behavior

FIVE

Understanding Heroic Behavior

J ohn would not remember his dinner that evening, not in light of everything they had spoken about. He felt eager to start implementing the concepts of the Heroic Environment, but he had one overriding concern he couldn't shake.

Kip, on the other hand, seemed to be enjoying every morsel of his pot roast. He joked with the waiter as if they were old friends and kept the conversation light, deflecting John's attempts to return to their ongoing discussion.

Finally, Kip put his fork down, drained his glass of water, folded his napkin on the table, and said, "John, you look perplexed. What is it?"

"Kip, I'm overwhelmed. I'd like to institute the principles of the Heroic Environment, like we discussed earlier, but how do I get started? I mean, they're great building blocks if the whole organization implements them. But how does someone like me, who is not the company's president or even the plant manager, start instituting change within an organization that hasn't agreed to act heroically? I feel as though I've been given a blueprint without a set of instructions or materials."

Kip nodded. "You're right, of course. The Heroic Environment cannot be instituted until management and staff are committed to it. But in the meantime, there is a way to begin on a more realistic, individual level. You can start with the group of employees you are directly responsible for, whether they number one or fifty. You first have to build a basic level of agreement among this small group, and that agreement has to do with the way you treat them and the way they respond in kind.

"There are five individual behavior traits involved. Together I call these five traits **Heroic Behavior**." Kip turned his place mat over and quickly penned the five traits.

HEROIC BEHAVIOR TRAITS

1. *Give and receive permission to act with autonomy.*
2. *Treat others as significant.*
3. *Make everyone feel like an insider.*
4. *Trust first and expect others to trust you in return.*
5. *Act with integrity.*

John studied the paper. "So starting with Heroic Behavior can eventually lead to the creation of the Heroic Environment?"

"Exactly! It's a modest way of beginning, but it *will* work. What eventually happens is that when you put Heroic Behavior into action in your office or department, you start a process that eventually gets noticed by others. And the ball begins to roll.

"But let's talk about the first trait, **give and receive permission to act with autonomy**," said Kip. "It's amazing how many

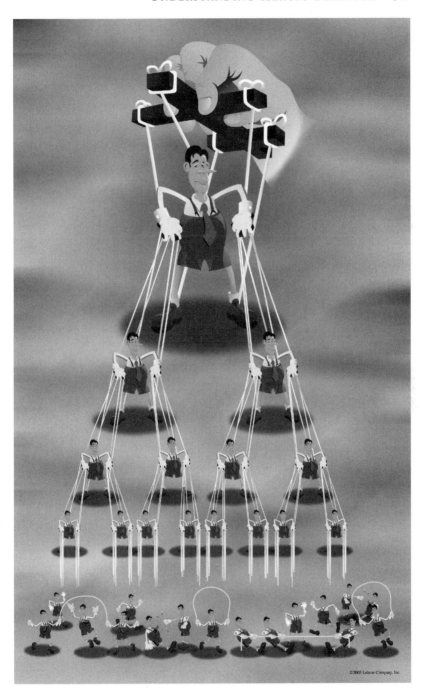

managers tend to overmanage their employees. They don't seem to realize that by constantly hovering over their staff they're suffocating their employees' creativity and sense of adulthood and creating a self-fulfilling prophecy. When people aren't given the chance to act responsibly, out of their own choice, they don't— they act like children. Furthermore, overbearing managers kill the creativity that lies in most individuals. In fact, you might call the managers puppeteers because of the way they pull all the strings. But, don't forget, they too are puppets for someone else in the larger Pyramid."

"O.K, O.K," John jumped in, feeling acutely uncomfortable. "To some extent, you're describing me. I know that I tend to overmanage. But if I don't watch what my people are doing, how can I be responsible for the results?"

"I understand," Kip smiled sympathetically. "A good manager, like a good coach, has three tasks that must be done well. First, the manager must make sure that the group he or she is managing is good. Yogi Berra, the famous New York Yankee catcher and later manager, once said, 'Great managers become great when they have great players.' And he was right. Overmanaging is the kiss of death. Second, the manager should give the team a clear idea of the desired results. And last, the manager should give team members as much freedom as possible to succeed."

"But I don't trust all my people enough to give them complete freedom."

"John, the best managers and supervisors I know go by an old Chinese proverb: Only hire people you trust, but once you've hired them, trust them. Only in the case of failure to act should the manager ever consider reducing a team member's autonomy, and then only after lots of discussion. Even then, as soon as the staff member performs well, autonomy should be restored;

otherwise, the employee doesn't belong on the team or in the group. That may be hard for some organizations to swallow, but those are the facts.

"In my experience, the fear to act with autonomy is not about ability, experience, or character. It's about fear of failure. Everyone wants to succeed, at least that is what we must believe. So it's our job in supervision to create the conditions for their success. Taking responsibility for the actions of front-line folks is wrong, and trying to separate accountability and responsibility doesn't work either.

"One of the reasons teenagers and parents have such a rough go of it is that the parents want to hold on to the accountability and then expect their kids to be responsible. It just doesn't work that way. No, you've got to insist that every member of your team be both accountable and responsible for his or her decisions, actions, and behaviors. We're all going to make mistakes, plenty of them. And if a mistake is made, then we fix the mistake and learn from the experience; but if a person refuses to be responsible and accountable, he or she doesn't belong on the team."

"Wow," John said in astonishment, "it's so simple, isn't it? Why do we tend to make things so complicated?"

"John, overmanaged employees are like ships with ten years' growth of barnacles on the bottoms of their hulls. We sometimes say that if you're managing people, you've hired the wrong folks. Why watch people you trust? And if you don't trust them...well, you recognize the alternative. No, I'm for managers becoming Wise Counsels: supervisors and managers who have *resigned* from trying to control people. They're evolved leaders, at every level, who trust people because they know it's the only way to get results. A Wise Counsel's purpose and role is that of a coach and counselor helping integrate resources and supporting TransAction Points that are the responsibility of the Front-Line Worker. They're smart enough to know that they can not and should not own the outcome of a job or task that is performed by someone else. They never abandon Front-Line Workers, and they help everyone around them remove TransAction blocks that stand in the way of building great products and delivering on every customer's expectations." At that, Kip took out a graph showing the relationship between Wise Counsels and Front-Line Workers.

"Creating TransAction Zones is not a new idea. Great organizations around the world have naturally implemented TransAction Zones for years. Remember Nordstrom?"

"I sure do," said John.

Kip continued. "And, I might add, they just announced a 150 percent profit increase this last quarter. Not bad for an organization that believes in people and started as a single shoe store nearly 100 years ago."

"I know Nordstrom, and I know how they treat us. My wife loves the place. Sometimes I think I'll have to call out the National Guard to get her to leave the store," said John.

Kip laughed and remarked that he and his wife love the TransAction Zone experience at Nordstrom, too.

"You know, John," said Kip, "just about everyone who has shopped there has a Nordstrom story of their own. And the reason for this level of customer loyalty is that the employees care and are treated as autonomous thinking individuals. The Ritz-Carlton cares, too, and shows it by giving their chambermaids an overall $2,000 budget to make sure that each customer experience is a great one."

"Now that's the kind of TransAction Zone I could get used to!" said John.

"Yes, John, we all could, but note the astonishingly high level of trust given to the Front-Line Worker. And that seems to be the formula for success."

"Yes, but TransAction Zones are not only for service organizations are they, Kip?" John wondered.

"No, John, they work just as well in manufacturing, research, education, or even government environments. When people are trusted, that's the beginning of creating an effective TransAction Zone. And the processes, systems, policies, and standards don't drive the transAction. No, it's driven at the TransAction Point, where every interaction is a gift," said Kip.

"John, working this way garners better results, and the company grows faster as well. I once heard someone say, 'you can lead a thousand people, but you can't carry three on your back.'"

"It would be amusing if it didn't hit home so hard," said John, shaking his head and wondering how his work environment had gotten so far away from focusing on internal and external customers. Why did they, he wondered, abandon their belief in people as the solution and embrace round after round of incentive programs, new processes that were forced into his operation without anyone requesting these new programs and new management theories? The real answer lay dormant in a corner— just trust people to be great!

Kip continued. "The second trait is **treat others as significant**. People need to feel special and valued. What this means is that everyone in the work group is empowered with a sense of importance. Furthermore, they're taught how to show appreciation to fellow workers. To instill this behavior is quite easy. It simply has to start with you. You'll be amazed how quickly everyone catches on.

"This brings me to an interesting survey you may have heard about. Nearly twenty years ago, the U.S. Chamber of Commerce conducted a study on what employees want. They proceeded to show both employees and managers ten priorities and asked them to rate them from 1 to 10, with 1 being the most important. Let me show you the results." Kip reached into his coat pocket and removed a folded piece of paper.

WHAT DO EMPLOYEES WANT?

Items Rated by Employees and Employers	Rated by Employees (in order of importance)	Rated by Management (in order of importance)
1 · Appreciation	1	8
2 · Feeling "in" on things	2	10
3 · Help on personal problems	3	9
4 · Job security	4	2
5 · Good wages	5	1
6 · Interesting work	6	5
7 · Promotions	7	3
8 · Management loyalty to workers	8	6
9 · Good working conditions	9	4
10 · Tactful disciplining	10	7

Source: U.S. Chamber of Commerce© 1986. The Balanced Program.

"Notice how far apart employees and managers are from each other."

John let out a low whistle. "Why is that?"

"Perhaps it's because our managers are taught principles that no longer apply today. The reason employees don't put good wages as their number one priority is that they take a decent wage for granted—we're no longer working in sweatshops. The new breed of employee is looking for more than good wages; today's employee is seeking to be a part of an extended family of productive people, where everyone matters. And if you look at our younger workers, it's even more true.

"Yet even today, you still hear some managers say, 'If so and so doesn't like it here, let him go elsewhere.' What foolish arrogance! Good employees are a company's most important assets! John, people are not renewable resources. In a Heroic Environment, there is no *us* versus *them* mentality. Hierarchies are deemphasized. Everyone uses the term "we" when talking about the company.

"This leads me to the third trait of Heroic Behavior, **make everyone feel like an insider**. People need to feel that they belong, that they have insider status in their workplace. Otherwise, they feel alienated."

"I'm not sure I have a handle on how this works," said John.

Kip thought for a moment. "Okay, here's a good example of how *not* to treat people. In the '70s and early '80s, as Detroit was seeing its market share eroding quickly to foreign car manufacturers, panic set in, with everyone blaming others for the problem. One plant manager decided that the problem was one of image. So he issued a memo forbidding those employees not driving a company-manufactured car from parking in the salaried employees' and guests' parking lot. 'This condition does not convey a positive image to other salaried employees or guests who visit our plant,' the memo stated, 'and it has a negative impact on our share of the car market. Henceforth, salaried workers driving the offending cars will be banished to the hourly workers' lot.'

"Now, as you know, the hourly workers are generally the assembly workers—people with more direct contact with building the cars than the secretaries, managers, accountants, and other salaried staff. And they were offended. Here's what the vice president of the local union said: 'They are punishing the salaried employees by telling them to park with my people, as if *we* were dogs. A lot of us consider this offensive.'"

"I bet the union had a field day with that one!" John exclaimed gleefully.

"Yes, I'm sure they did, but that's not the point. The point is that the plant's most important assets, the people who build its cars, were treated like outsiders by an unthinking manager. It's not as if the Front-Line Workers weren't concerned about the company's problems—over a third of their friends had already lost their jobs.

"But nobody likes to feel like a second-class citizen. I believe that people want to be part of building something important. And they want to be *in* on decisions. That's why smart managers bring their people together to discuss problems. Often, it's the hands-on people who have the solutions. *Involve employees in finding solutions, and you've unleashed an invaluable resource.*"

"I think there's another way employees are left outside," added John. "In my company, I see new employees given very little instruction and then their managers wait for them to make a mistake, which is then corrected. It is almost like the fraternity ritual of hazing: Make the task as hard as possible and see who survives."

"Yes, it's a form of withholding information, and most non-Heroic companies practice it. It's often not a conscious act, just a relic of a more oppressive past. Mentoring people from the very beginning is so important. Teach them the ropes properly, and you'll find yourself doing a lot of praising instead of criticizing.

"John, there's a saying that 'information is power.' Many try to withhold it and believe that by doing so they become more powerful. Ironically, the reverse is true. The most powerful people throughout the ages were the men and women who *freely* gave of their knowledge. In fact, in our information age, the more information you can share with more people, the more powerful you and your group become. But sadly, that's not what we do. I call this the real tragedy of working in a Pyramid."

John sat silently. Some of what he was hearing was painful because it revealed his failings. He had always considered himself a good manager; now he wasn't sure. Finally, he said, "I never realized before to what extent what I practice reflects who I *am,* and that it affects everyone that works for me. What a responsibility!"

Kip smiled. "Well, I have something that will cheer you up." He motioned to the waiter and ordered strawberry shortcake for both of them.

"It's not exactly on my diet, but we've been working overtime, so let's splurge a little," Kip said, with a wide grin. Listening to Kip's cheerful talk helped John relax. He realized how important it was to him to earn Kip's respect. And Kip's nonjudgmental attitude toward him was a lesson in mentoring all by itself.

As their dessert was served, both John and Kip took the opportunity to enjoy the sound of the rumbling train. There was something soothing about the distant cacophony of steel rolling over iron.

Finally, Kip settled back in his seat and began discussing the fourth trait of Heroic Behavior. "**Trust first and expect others to trust you in return** acts as an empowering message to others. In an atmosphere thick with suspicion, everyone is afraid to act spontaneously. As a result, the organization becomes inflexible and brittle. It cannot adjust quickly to change.

"Trust, on the other hand, is the darnedest thing. It's hard to define, and so many people talk about it, yet few know how to offer it to others. I think that's because trust is the most Heroic of all traits. You really have to overcome the fear of having your trust betrayed to risk trusting others. It's a little like jumping into the darkness with the confidence that someone will be there to catch you—that's Heroic.

"Is it worth it? Absolutely, because a team that trusts its members will always out-achieve a team that's ruled by distrust and intimidation. Nontrusting organizations create multiple Pyramids to maintain control while holding onto their false powers. And they do this by using manipulative tactics such as reward and punishment programs, instead of trusting people."

"But why is that?" asked John.

"It goes back to a different belief system about managing people. In the early '60s, the buzzword was 'MBO—Management by Objective.' This was a concept about how to delegate tasks and achieve results, and managers got all excited about it because this allowed them to deal with numbers and not with employees. Senior managers, many of whom had been military officers accustomed to giving orders and not expecting feedback, had seen results in this command-and-control environment, and so they transferred this approach to industry."

"Here we go again with the chimpanzee story," said John, half joking and half serious.

"Yes, I'm afraid so!" said Kip. "These managers were comfortable with wielding power and having control over others without being questioned. So, of course, they got excited about a system that gave them a measurable way to control the people they managed without having to partner with their people — people who, deep down, they did not regard as equals anyway. It was a foolproof accountability system—or so they thought. The only problem was, this widely accepted technique didn't take into consideration how people really *want* to be treated and how they perform best. Take a look at this graph that the English magazine *The Economist* put together to show the slide in profits

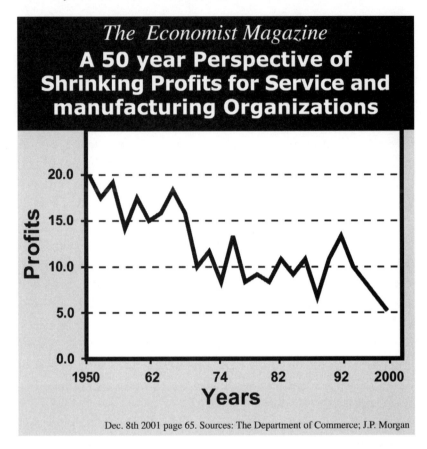

The Economist Magazine
A 50 year Perspective of Shrinking Profits for Service and manufacturing Organizations

Dec. 8th 2001 page 65. Sources: The Department of Commerce; J.P. Morgan

since all these modern management practices—that discounted the power of the individual and only recognized the importance of systems and processes—came into favor.

"The chart begins with 1950 and extends for fifty years. I think it will shock you. Note how profits have been destroyed by these practices. Some might suggest that competition undermined profitability, but their observation would be incorrect. No, the facts speak for themselves. Over the past fifty years, management practices have undermined profits...not competitors or foreign products.

"Economists who have seen this trend are recognizing something even deeper and more foreboding if this trend continues. We must make a major shift regarding our assumptions about our enterprise-wide strategic thinking. During the past fifty years, industry and service environments have emphasized capital investment and size as the most important currency for an operation's success."

As John studied the chart, Kip broke the silence. "But no one was keeping score regarding this newly emerging trend of the post-World War II era of trusting systems rather than peoples' good efforts. Business schools began teaching delegation skills, command-and-control leadership, branding techniques, management by objective, and new process designs.

"So the next thing we knew, everyone was delegating and managing by objective, while no one was extending or lavishing trust. Instead the theories contradicted everything that made practical sense. We in top management were hell-bent on controlling every nickel and acting like cops, measuring everything that moved and incentivizing like crazy. And to make matters worse, the system included penalties for failure, all without any input from the poor devils who had to live under this 'great, new, modern system' that they had no say in. At that point, we had entered the era of hermetically sealed management," said Kip, smiling sadly. "In a tragic way, people were losing faith in each other and embracing measurements and incentive programs with a death grip. We had created so many strings and controls that we were choking.

"The major problem with all this was that we were imposing systems on people who had no control over their own production practices, quality levels, or design features. Instead of creating the right measures, measures to study an operation's capacities and the customer's various needs, we were counting beans. Crunching numbers and hitting abstract goals became all-important.

Balancing scorecards and meeting crazy quotas was the game. We had let loose a monster we seemingly couldn't stop. Some so-called experts actually believed that since robots would eventually take over factory tasks anyway, as well as answer phones and take orders on-line, there was no reason to be concerned about people issues, the issues they had dubbed 'the soft skills.' And the exporting of jobs became the rage.

"You can pretty much trace America's competitive decline during the '80s and '90s to the mentality of that time, and many operations still haven't changed their thinking. Thank heaven other operations are finally now abandoning these failed notions. This post-World War II trend is over and the new trend is to invest in people. Moving from large capital investments to investing in people is beginning to make sense again."

"I understand," responded John, "but surely we need standards. How do we achieve results without controlling people through measurements?"

Kip was waiting for this question. "John, we develop standards and high quality service levels by *developing responsibility throughout the entire organization*. After thirty years of grappling with this very subject, I am convinced that the individuals and groups that are accountable for the transAction must also be responsible for their decisions. *Separating these two issues is the kiss of death.* That way, people take on the role of quality control while they measure what really matters—the flow of work and the satisfaction of the customers they serve. And all the evidence shows that, with few exceptions, people who have been extended trust—both responsibility and accountability—will naturally exhibit new and higher standards of work quality, ethical behavior, fairness, personal autonomy, and creativity. Heck, if you want innovation to appear in your work environment—at every level—you can't get there by creating a Pyramid approach. It's just delusional thinking!"

John felt elated. "I've got it! It's so simple!"

"It may be simple," Kip cautioned the younger man, "but it isn't easy! It's not just that managers who have decided not to be cops have to reorient their thinking. Employees who were treated like objects have to release their own defense mechanisms and willingly assume responsibility and accountability for their actions, decisions, and performance. It doesn't happen overnight, and it may take twice as long as you would like, but once it begins it is darn near infinite!"

"How do you know when you're succeeding?" John wondered aloud.

"One way is when you start hearing over and over from job applicants that they've heard about your organization's great working conditions—and that they heard about it from your employees! That's when you know your team members are acting as the company's ambassadors and that things are starting to gel."

Capitalizing on the momentum of the conversation, Kip continued. "Now, the fifth trait of Heroic Behavior is just as important: **Act with integrity.**"

"I hear that word so often I no longer know what it means. What's your definition of integrity?" asked John.

"Integrity deals with the most far-reaching question of all. It constantly asks the critical question, 'What does our office, our group, or our organization stand for?' "

John looked perplexed.

"Let me tell you a story that will explain this," said Kip. "Not long ago, the CEO of a company and a group of his senior managers were all together in a product-planning meeting. The topic was the shipping date of a new product the company had been working on for two years. There was a pile of purchase orders waiting to be filled and articles about the product had been written in industry magazines. Industry-wide anticipation was high. Furthermore, with all the advance orders, if the product could be shipped by the end of the quarter, the company would reach the sales and profit figures it had promised Wall Street, and the CEO would be the darling of his board of directors.

"But there was a problem. The head of product development said there were glitches with the product, and that it would not be ready for shipment by the end of the quarter. The CEO hit the roof. Something had to be done! In his best management-by-objectives style, he asked what other product could be shipped instead. The head of product development said there was an earlier version of the product that had several unsolved bugs, but it could be resurrected. That was the only alternative."

"So what happened?" asked John, shaking his head and knowing that this was the making of a first-class scandal.

"The CEO ordered the old prototype be shipped."

"But why didn't he realize the long-term consequences?" asked John.

"It was because he didn't want to be skewered by Wall Street." Kip paused. "Yes, John, the CEO wasn't a stupid man, just a foolish one. These folks believed that they had to meet their financial numbers for the blasted quarter, regardless.

"Now, the story really heats up. When production heard that the defective product was going to be shipped, they couldn't believe their ears. I mean pandemonium broke out in every corner of the plant: Quality control was insulted because their concerns were overridden even after impassioned emails had been circulated. They were embarrassed by the whole affair and knew that this decision would unleash catastrophe—but no one was listening up top.

"Customer support was outraged. They knew they'd be victimized in a war between unhappy customers and their company, and that they would be blamed for not being able to soothe the customers. And sales, after initial elation that back orders would be filled, realized that selling a defective product would damage their relationship with their customers for a long time and ultimately drive some customers away—but they would get their bonus for the year, and to some, that was the silver lining to their short-term thinking."

"I can't believe all these problems weren't seen before this decision was made," John said. "Are you sure this really happened?"

"Oh, there's more," said Kip, smiling like he had just swallowed a canary. "Public relations was the last to find out about management's plan. They were *really* in a bind. Should they deny the allegations about a shoddy product—knowing that emails were now floating outside the organization—or should they admit that a defective product had been released, thus setting up top management for the fall? If they admitted the product's faults, they would have to answer to the public and press. Or, if they denied the product was shoddy, they would risk personal and professional loss of reputation in the future and even legal action by the Federal Trade Commission. Their careers hung in the balance. Not only that, but if they coordinated their answers with other corporate departments, they could even be accused of willful wrongdoing and illegal conspiracy.

"Well, John, as you can see, one decision at the highest level to achieve some numerical goal to look good for the short-term was costing the organization its integrity, reputation, and soul. Instead of Heroically telling the truth by announcing to everyone that the product would be shipping late—because their first objective was to offer great products to the public—the company squandered the trust of its employees, its vendors, and the public."

John just sat in his seat shaking his head in disbelief. But Kip wasn't through with his lesson and wanted to add substance to his young friend's evening. Kip pulled out another piece of paper from his briefcase to show John.

Why Companies Lose Customers

Influenced by friends	5%
Lured away by competition	9%
TURNED AWAY BY AN ATTITUDE OF INDIFFERENCE	68%
Dissatisfied with the product	14%
Moved away	3%
Died	1%

"Here's a research project that emphasizes why customers leave. The American Society for Quality Control (ASQC) reports that the following study shows the relative importance of the top six reasons companies lose customers.

"The amazing bottom-line fact is that nowhere in modern management books or graduate schools does it suggest that nearly 70 percent of the time the reason companies lose customers is *indifference*. Not one book suggests that this is the case. Instead, they always point to problems in pricing, supply-chain dynamics, incentive programs, advertising, management style, branding, positioning, technology, innovation, momentum, etc., etc.—but *never indifference!* People need to be part of something they can feel proud of, or they will distance themselves from the product and the company they're supposed to represent," Kip said with emphasis.

John broke his trance to reflect back on the story of the CEO releasing a shoddy product. "No wonder so many employees perceive senior management as being dishonest and incompetent!" exclaimed the younger man. "By the way, what happened to the turnover at the company?"

"You mean the Chapter 11 reorganization? Not long after the press lost interest in the story, the organization filed for bankruptcy. I think that's what you'd call 'major turnover.' And, oh, you'll get a laugh out of this. The board of directors had created a severance package for the CEO, and he walked out with over $17 million in bonuses!" Kip just shook his head in disgust.

"John, remember this well: when it comes to integrity, there are no shortcuts. As you move up the ranks, as I'm sure you will, there will be times when the pressure will be on you to perform, to achieve a goal, and you'll be tempted to take a shortcut. When that time comes, remember this moment and do the right thing.

"But let me apply this behavior to your situation today. Suppose you're enacting Heroic Behavior with your group, and your company asks you to do something that you consider unethical. Would you do it?"

John thought for a long while. "First, I would have to be certain in my mind that the order is really unethical, as opposed to one I disagree with. After all, as a member of the corporate team, I must execute many decisions I may not agree with. However, if after much soul-searching I become certain it is a matter of ethics, I would use every available channel to voice my objections to my superiors."

"And risk your chances for advancement, even your job?" Kip interjected.

"Yes."

"Suppose they ignore your opposition?" pressed Kip.

"Then I would have no choice but to resign."

"You mean you'd risk losing everything you've worked for, just for the sake of your integrity and reputation?"

"Everything I've worked for would be worth *nothing* without my integrity," John replied.

The silence seemed never-ending as Kip just smiled with pride.

Chapter Six

The Four Corporate Personality Work Styles

SIX

The Four Corporate Personality Work Styles

As the two men returned to their compartment, John pulled a blank pad from his briefcase and wrote some notes about their dinner conversation. He wanted to make sure he wouldn't forget what he was learning. The five Heroic Behavior Traits struck both an emotional and a rational chord, and it made sense that developing this kind of behavior would be a good first step toward creating a Heroic Environment. Yet even as he was writing, new questions were begging to be answered.

"Kip, I'm afraid you aren't quite rid of me...do you mind?"

"Not at all," said Kip, putting down his newspaper. "I'm just surprised you don't want to take a break from all this."

"I can't," the younger man blurted out. Then, as he realized how intense he'd sounded, he smiled self-consciously. Kip returned his smile, and John relaxed.

"Okay, I think I understand Heroic Behavior. Heroic Behavior creates an atmosphere where people can act Heroically, doesn't it?"

Kip nodded.

"Then would you please give me your definition of a Hero?"

"Sure," said Kip, "let me start by telling you about someone I admire very much. I once worked with Max, a very special man. He had an uncanny ability to cut right to the heart of a problem by understanding the human factors behind it. And when he would solve a problem, he would do it with everyone's ego intact. He seemed to know exactly how to treat others.

"Max had a gift for understanding human needs. He reinforced his coworkers' senses of self-esteem without appearing insincere. He made everyone feel important. Even if he disagreed with someone, that person would walk away from him feeling more focused and inspired. He knew how to keep the discussion on the issues, never attacking a person's sense of dignity in the process.

"At the time I was working with him, I was young and worked long hours. I thought pretty highly of myself. And yet I wasn't getting half the bottom-line results Max was. One day, utterly frustrated, I cornered him and asked directly about his success. His answer was simple: 'Kip, I put the needs of others before my own.'

"Frankly, I didn't buy it—his answer seemed far too altruistic. I dismissed his words, but I couldn't dismiss his ongoing success. I saw how his influence grew without him seeming to work at it. So I started to take more notice, and you know what? Max was right. It *was* his genuine interest in others and how others responded to him that made the difference.

"He had other virtues. He would stand up for the things and the people he believed in without fear. When necessary, he would take charge, yet he much preferred to let his employees try their hand at leadership. He was the first Wise Counsel I ever met. At times, he would roll up his sleeves and become just one of the team members. As a result, those around him became experienced and confident leaders themselves. And, of course, by developing a team of capable, enthusiastic people, Max used minimal time supervising and maximum time creating and producing. Where I was spending 60 percent of my time making sure my team got the job done, he was spending only 10 percent—and getting better results.

"John, you should have seen his genuine happiness when he saw his coworkerssucceeding. He was so optimistic, yet he wasn't the least bit naïve. He could smell a phony a mile away."

"So *that's* your model for the Hero," exclaimed John.

"Guilty as charged," Kip answered good-naturedly. "But let's generalize our discussion so that it can apply anywhere.

"Heroes make things happen. They are the men and women who tend to focus on finding solutions while others are still defining the problem. They are results-oriented, not process-oriented. And because of their can-do attitude, they move the whole organization forward. A Hero's motto is, 'It doesn't matter who gets the credit as long as the job gets done.' And because they are *results-driven*, not ego-driven, they tend to throw the limelight on others. Yet, paradoxically, Heroes become immensely powerful in a positive way. Why? Because their motives are universally trusted.

"Heroes are also facilitators of new ideas. When they discover a beneficial idea, they champion it, regardless of its source. And then they fight for its success by working toward reaching a consensus.

"The most important value of Heroes is that they create a model of behavior for others to emulate. They bring out the best in people and, as such, define the direction of the team."

As Kip was talking, he noticed a crestfallen look on John's face. John seemed distracted and fidgety. "What's wrong, John?" he asked.

Looking at Kip, John shook his head. "The more you describe the Hero, the less confident I am that I could be like that. Look," he said, with an edge in his voice, "I try to put the interests of others before my own, but I don't always succeed. Nor do I often stand up for unpopular ideas in meetings, even if I agree with them…I haven't always acted courageously."

Kip understood. "Don't be so hard on yourself. Acting Heroically is a process. None of us succeeds all the time, but it's a model for which we strive. And when we stray from it, we can return to it *at any time.*"

"Okay, I can accept that," John answered, "but there's another question that's been bothering me. Can you honestly expect every member of the Heroic Environment to become a Hero in the way you just defined? What about the difference in personalities, capabilities, capacity, and even commitment?

"Most experts agree that our personality is a mix of our genetic makeup and our life experiences, especially our childhood experiences. Our personality emerges as we make our way in this world. Some of us want to be liked and accepted, while others don't seem to care what others think about them. Some are compelled to become leaders, while others prefer to follow. The complexity and variety of human behavior is amazing. So it's important not to *judge* people for being who they are. By the time people come into the workplace, they have developed a set of behavior patterns that affect they way they work. I call this a person's **Dominant Work Style**.

"Over the years, I've found it extremely useful to think in terms of four Dominant Work Styles interacting in an organization: the **Hero**, the **Maverick**, the **9-to-5-er**, and the **Dissident**.

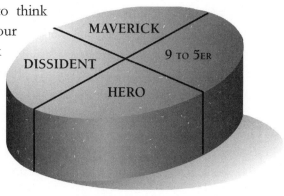

"I've already described my idea of the Hero, so let me tell you about the **Maverick**. Mavericks are noted for coming up with new ideas, methods, and strategies. Their ideas keep an organization or group competitive and challenged. They are the original thinkers—the poets. They represent our creative best—what we can become if we allow ourselves to dream and imagine.

"Mavericks deal with the world in two ways. Either they welcome controversy as they flaunt their disregard for what others think—I'm sure you can think of some performers and artists as well as entrepreneurs who might fall into this category—or, as happens much more often, they are the poets, the dreamers, the philosophers, the scientists, and the thinkers—the people who often withdraw into their own world. These creative types have learned to live without a great need for group acceptance. They are in the habit of developing new ideas on their own. Because society has always treated them as 'different,' they're often mistrustful of others and may not be good at getting their ideas across.

"Mavericks are some of my favorite people, mind you. Most of us believe that old saying, 'If it ain't broke, don't fix it,' until our competition leaves us in the dust. Mavericks keep us on our toes by insisting that just because 'it ain't broke' doesn't mean we shouldn't try to make it better. Of course, no one likes to hear this, so Mavericks often end up in hot water because some in power may interpret their new ideas or differing opinions as a challenge to their leadership. How unfortunate!

"The truth is, when an organization is in crisis, it probably is a Maverick who bails it out with an original solution. So when an organization listens to its Mavericks, it safeguards against corporate failure and ensures long-term success." Kip's emphatic tone told John that he was speaking from personal experience.

John wanted to make sure he understood the Maverick. "Are Mavericks, then, the complainers, the people who play devil's advocate?"

"Not at all. They're independent thinkers who may see a different solution from the rest of the group. For them, the issue isn't dissent. Because they have vision, they look to more far-reaching solutions to problems than the majority. If they have to complain or play devil's advocate, they will, but for them the only issue is getting the best results possible."

"Does that mean that we must always accept the opinion of Mavericks?"

"Of course not. Mavericks often come up with highly impractical ideas. The key is to learn to listen with an open mind before judging the merit of an idea. Furthermore, it's important to recognize how much courage it takes to be a Maverick."

"Courage? Why courage?" asked John.

"Have you ever stood up and offered an opinion at a meeting?" asked Kip.

"Sure, but I was always uncomfortable until I saw how people responded to it."

"Meaning that if your idea was liked, you relaxed again?"

John nodded.

"Now, imagine spending your life offering proposals and ideas that are frequently rejected. If you have the guts to get up again and again and propose new ideas, don't you think you would be courageous?"

"I see your point, Kip."

"All right, now that we understand the major traits of a Maverick, let's discuss the **9-to-5-er**."

John smiled a slightly disparaging smile, which did not escape Kip's notice.

"Because of the term I use for them, you might think I don't respect 9-to-5-ers," Kip said, eyeing John intently. "Nothing could be farther from the truth. The historian Will Durant explained it best. He said the story of humankind is like a river. The major personalities and events are like torrents that sweep everything into their wake. But on the banks of a river are the villagers who live their lives, raise their families, grow their food, regardless of what heroic or terrible events occur around them.

"Think of the 9-to-5-ers as these villagers. They are involved in building a better life for themselves and their families. While they're at work, they work. And if you give them good instructions and treat them with respect, they do a good job.

"But for them, work is not everything. They balance their life between work and play. They are devoted parents, and they have a strong sense of community. But if you ever need them, they'll go the extra mile for you, as long as you treat them with the respect they deserve.

"9-to-5-ers are also the most influenced by their working environment. They can be either motivated or apathetic—it all depends on the way they're treated. It also takes courage to be a 9-to-5-er."

John wasn't convinced. "Why would you call 9-to-5-ers courageous?"

"Let me answer you with a little story. Not long ago I sat by a young woman on an airplane. Her name was Cynthia. Her company was sending her to a computer course to learn new skills in her area—inventory control. I asked her about her job and her life. She told me she was divorced with two young children. She was a devoted mother who was frustrated because she didn't always have the time she wanted for the kids, but she did her best. She held a full-time job and commuted every day for an hour each way. In addition, she was going to school one night a week. Even though she obviously had a number of priorities beyond work, she was willing to learn new skills that would help her company. Now I ask you, wouldn't you consider Cynthia courageous?"

John picked up Kip's thread. "I see what you mean. Like the unsung heroes of wartime, 9-to-5-ers may not set the world on fire with their leadership or creativity, but day-in and day-out they carry out the work they're assigned without complaint. Without them, the organization would sputter and come to a halt."

John remained silent for a while. He was beginning to realize that deep respect and inclusion for *all* people is the foundation of the Heroic Environment. He remembered recent incidents where he might have been abrupt with some of his plant workers, and he felt inwardly embarrassed. He resolved to not let that happen again.

Finally, his attention returned to his conversation with Kip. "Tell me about the last Dominant Work Style—the **Dissident**."

"Ah, yes, the Dissident…an integral part of every organization," Kip said thoughtfully. "But before I talk about the Dissident, I'd like to make three points. First, unlike the other Dominant Work Styles, which are peoples' basic personalities, the Dissident is often created by circumstances in the workplace. Second, the Dissident is the only one of the four that is essentially negative. And third, and most important, I want to make sure you understand that acting as a Dissident is not the same as expressing a dissenting opinion.

"In the Heroic Environment, dissenting opinions are actively encouraged, even sought after. An honest difference of opinion is vital to the survival and success of any organization. The key to honest dissent is that the disagreement is born out of a genuine desire to help the group achieve its goals. On the other hand, the Dissident, as I define it here, is a person who no longer roots for the team's success."

"Why wouldn't someone want to see his own team win?" asked John.

"There are several reasons. A Dissident could be a former Maverick whose proposal was rejected for someone else's and who now is hoping that the accepted proposal will fail. Or he could be a 9-to-5-er who feels that his leaders are not 'walking the talk' and is therefore bitter. Or the Dissident could be a fallen Hero who cannot accept the authority of another leader."

"I see," interrupted John. "People who no longer see themselves as *part* of the team may become Dissidents."

"That's it in a nutshell!" said Kip, impressed with John's insight.

"Then when we see dissident behavior, the appropriate response is to find out what is causing the behavior and help that person feel part of the team once again," responded John. "It all goes back to the Heroic Behavior of *helping people feel like insiders,* doesn't it?"

Kip nodded.

"The way I see it," John continued, "we all feel outside the team sometimes. The worst possible thing to do would be to further isolate the Dissident."

"Well done, John. You're on the right track. The best way to help Dissidents is to embrace them and bring them back on board. Of course, this doesn't always work. Ultimately, Dissidents themselves must recognize their own counterproductive behavior."

John looked perplexed, so Kip continued. "Let me tell you a story to illustrate what I mean.

"Two partners, Alan and Peter, who together had built an advertising agency, were at a point where their differences had pretty nearly destroyed their relationship. In the early years, they were inseparable and their business had grown and prospered. They had genuinely liked and enjoyed each other. Often, in the middle of a sales presentation, one would finish the other's sentence.

"But with the passage of time, that all changed. Both men came to dwell upon the other's shortcomings, missed opportunities, blind spots, and vulnerabilities. Instead of acting Heroically and putting the other's interests first, their bickering turned ugly. In fact, they communicated with each other mostly through their administrative assistants, who had nicknamed the situation 'The Cold War.'

"Alan was the older of the two and served as head copywriter for the agency. He had a sharp wit, was a natty dresser, and demanded perfection from his staff. Peter, a free spirit, was the creative director. His suits never seemed pressed and his style was imprecise, but his employees and clients loved him for his spontaneity and gift for design. Each man's strengths matched the other's weaknesses.

"Because of their Cold War though, the entire agency suffered. Employees were actively taking sides, with the popular Peter definitely winning the loyalty of the agency. Alan was feeling increasingly isolated at his own company.

"One day, the agency was invited to present its work to a potentially major client who'd been on their dream list for years. Here was their big chance, and it couldn't have happened at a more critical time. Their Cold War had taken its toll, and the company was in dire straits financially. Getting this account could save their agency.

"The prospect's offices were in New Jersey, which meant traveling across the Hudson River from New York. Peter insisted on driving his new car and promised to pick up Alan at his New York City apartment at 10:30 A.M. sharp, giving them plenty of time to arrive at their noon presentation. Alan relented uneasily, knowing that Peter tended to run late.

"On Saturday morning, Alan was waiting at the curb ten minutes early. Ten-thirty came and went, no Peter. By 10:45, Alan was nervous and upset. By 11:00, he was contemplating murder."

John chuckled.

"Finally, at 11:10, Peter pulled up, completely unruffled at being forty minutes late. Alan, losing every vestige of self-control, started screaming at Peter, 'You've made us miss the presentation! I knew I shouldn't have trusted you! Now, we'll never make it on time.'

"Peter calmly turned to Alan and said, 'Don't worry, I've got a shortcut!'

"'A what?' shrieked Alan. 'A shortcut,' said Peter. 'In fact, that's why I'm late—I was getting the directions. This shortcut will cut nearly twenty-five minutes from the drive, so we have plenty of time.'

"As he entered the car, Alan was still bristling. For once, he wanted Peter to get his comeuppance. Suddenly, he had a realization. 'Good Heavens, what am I rooting for?' he thought. 'Am I hoping Peter's shortcut will work and get us there on time so we can get the account, or am I rooting for him to screw up in order to reinforce my beliefs that Peter's a fool who's responsible for all our problems?'"

"What happened? Did they get to the meeting on time?" John asked eagerly.

The older man paused for a moment. "You know, that's not the most important part of this story," he said, smiling. "What's important here is Alan's moment of truth, his realization that by focusing on his differences with Peter, he had lost sight of what was good for the agency. You see, what people root for is sometimes in conflict with their own best interest and the best interest of the team. After all, there were lots of people at the agency depending on these two for their livelihoods."

John went silent. The story of Alan and Peter affected him because he could see there had been a few times when he, too, had not rooted for his team's success, especially when he'd felt slighted by its leader. Was he a Dissident then? He started going over the four Work Styles in his mind. No, he concluded, he *couldn't* be a Dissident. The role of the Hero—helping, encouraging, and championing others—clearly attracted him the most. And he remembered Kip's comment that becoming a Hero was a never-ending process. He felt he had a long way to go.

Suddenly, John had new insight and with it, new questions. "Kip, you said each of us has a *Dominant* Work Style. Don't we use the other Work Styles as well? As I think about my experiences, I think I've used all four styles at one time or another."

"You know, John, you have a great deal of insight for someone so young," Kip responded. "You're right, of course. None of us is one-dimensional. In fact, have you ever noticed how many roles you play in a day? For example, when you return routine phone calls, you may be acting like any of the thousands of 9-to-5-ers. An hour later you may be backing a new proposal presented by an unpopular person solely because you see its merit. At that moment, you're acting like a Hero."

"I see what you mean," John said. "During the work day, I may change roles several times and use a different style."

"Right. And yet, for each of us there is a dominant style that defines our personality most of the time. But as the situation dictates, we may switch styles."

John nodded in understanding, but he wasn't yet satisfied. "Kip, we talked about Dissidents, and we agree that they should be made to feel part of the team again or that they need to have an insight into their own behavior. But what happens if, as happened to me, you have an employee who is so bent on the righteousness of his cause that he deliberately sabotages the organization's efforts?"

"Then you may have on your hands a more complex and dangerous situation," Kip answered gravely. "You may have encountered the type I call the **Terrorist**."

John's eyes widened as Kip continued. "There are some people—and they are few — who can never see themselves as part of the team. The reasons are complex, ranging from lack of family identification as children to a quiet sense of superiority to the group. It's not a healthy psychological state, and in the short run, it's not fixable.

"These people are Terrorists because of their behavior. For example, one may be a computer programmer who introduces a faulty program virus—just to destroy the work of others. Or another may engage in industrial espionage. They rationalize their behavior by creating in their minds wrongs and injustices that don't exist."

"Are there many Terrorists in a typical organization?"

"Fortunately, Terrorists are pretty rare. But their destructive abilities far exceed their numbers. Just read the daily paper."

John let out a low whistle.

Kip continued. "Great care must be taken before labeling someone a Terrorist. In fact, if you aren't careful with your labels, you could get yourself into a heap of trouble. Only extreme behavior would ever fall into this category."

"What do you do when you're absolutely positive that some-one is a Terrorist?" inquired John.

'If I were absolutely convinced that someone was acting in a way that was causing the organization definite harm, I would have to move for that person's dismissal. But again, you must be very careful to document your case with facts and not suspicions."

"Kip, you seem so cautious when talking about Terrorist behavior. Why?"

"Because all too often in autocratic organizations, people use labels to unjustly attack their enemies. If I'm reluctant to talk about this issue, it's because I'm sensitive to the injustices people have suffered because of their backgrounds or politics. Even in America, we had to deal with the McCarthy-era hysteria. People in an organization can also become paranoid and start labeling any-one who disagrees with authority as a Terrorist. So please, be care-ful with this one," Kip concluded emphatically.

John looked at his watch. It was almost 10:30 P.M.

"We'll be in Kansas City soon," Kip said with barely disguised excitement.

Both men decided to sit back and take a break. It took a moment before John remembered that Kansas City was where he was to meet Peggy Bentley, Kip's goddaughter and the *California Zephyr's* chief engineer for the next shift.

• • •

The train screeched to a halt, and the loudspeaker blared their arrival in Kansas City. Kip turned to John, "Better bring your overcoat. We'll have to get off the train and walk to the front to reach the engineer's compartment."

John inhaled the bracing air as they exited their car. It felt good, although the contrast to their warm compartment shocked his senses. The terminal seemed unusually busy for that time of night, with lots of sleepy children in the arms of their parents. John matched Kip's brisk pace through the scattered crowds. In spite of his years, Kip had the buoyant gait of someone half his age.

When they finally reached the engine, Kip called to Peggy as she was just about to board the train. They greeted each other affectionately. John waited for the two to catch up on family news, then Kip turned and introduced Peggy.

Peggy was in her mid-thirties. She had intelligent eyes and a professional way about her. As she shook John's hand, Kip briefed Peggy on his conversation with John since leaving the Chicago station earlier that day.

Peggy smiled a smile of recognition. "So what do you think of the Heroic Environment?"

"I think it's the most important concept I've ever heard," John replied with great enthusiasm.

Peggy's face turned serious. "Well, they certainly don't teach these kinds of ideas in business school, but I hope they will someday because they work."

"How do you know?" asked John.

"Because Kip helped my father institute the Heroic Environment concepts in his manufacturing business, and they've been a guiding light for him and for our entire family ever since."

"What made you decide to become a railroad engineer...I mean, it's not the typical career...."

"You mean for a woman, don't you?" Peggy said, laughing. "I'm afraid Kip is responsible for that, too. I've always loved trains, and Kip encouraged me to pursue my dream, even though it was unconventional."

"So now that you've achieved your goal..."

"I haven't achieved my goal," interrupted Peggy. "My goal is to bring back rail travel as a major way of transporting people. We're a long way from that, and yet our highways are becoming more and more crowded and our air more polluted. But I'm gratified to see how many people are coming back to train travel. One day, I hope we'll use it here as much as it's used in other developed countries like Japan, France, and Germany."

"And how do you propose to achieve this?" John asked, fascinated.

"I want to keep reinforcing the progress we're making by helping institute a Heroic Environment here. And to do this properly, I hope one day to become a leader and spokesperson for the rail industry."

"Wow, you certainly know what you want," John said, a bit enviously.

"Don't you, John?" Peggy asked.

"I'm still working on it," confided John, suddenly feeling like a high school freshman.

Kip, who had been listening to the exchange with keen interest, jumped in. "I have no doubts that John will make important contributions to his industry. But for now, we all must board the train."

For the first time that day, John noticed that Kip was weary. It had been a long and exciting day. After saying their goodbyes to Peggy, Kip and John returned to their compartment. Their bunks had been turned down for the night. They both agreed to continue their discussion in the morning.

Chapter Seven

Telling Someone You're Sorry

Telling Someone You're Sorry

As the train picked up speed leaving the Kansas City station, John knew that he and Kip had agreed to end the discussion for the night. But deep in his heart, he still had one burning, unanswered question. It kept creeping back into his mind, and he knew that unless he got an answer, his conscience would keep him awake. John decided he needed to ask one more question of his mentor before they turned in for the night.

"Kip, I'm sorry to bother you, but I've been thinking about a situation I have facing me when I return to work on Monday, and it's troubling me."

Kip turned toward John while slowly unfolding his pajamas. He realized that the younger man was carrying a burden and the weight was taking its toll. "John, it sounds important, so why don't you tell me about it and let's see if we can figure out what to do before we get some sleep?"

John took a deep breath and began. "Kip, it started late last year. I was introduced to the head of another department at work that was producing parts similar to those produced by my division. This fellow and I hit it off right away. I guess you could say that we had a lot of the same values. But early on, something went haywire.

"In looking back at the situation, I guess I appeared stubborn and assertive about my position and ideas. As you already know, depending upon the situation, I'm not afraid to speak my mind and to stand up for what I believe. Sometimes it's a little much for those around me. And in this case, it was about how an existing product could be built better and what features it would offer.

"The other fellow had also built a similar product for years at another organization and was rightfully proud of his techniques and experience. From my perspective, I expected him to come over to my way of thinking and I tried to communicate that belief.

"In our last get-together, I really blew it. We were supposed to work on a joint project, but the fellow felt so put off by my approach that I received a letter from him after our last meeting expressing his frustration, anger, and hurt feelings. He even went so far as to terminate our joint project."

Kip could see that John felt badly about the situation. Carefully, Kip began in a slow and deliberate manner to help John sort through his dilemma. "Whew! It sounds like the other fellow was pretty upset with you. For whatever it's worth, I'll bet the other fellow might also like to smooth out the situation.

"But first, let's step back from the sparks and concentrate on the substance of your comments and the disagreement. What did you say that caused such a reaction, and how did you act?" Kip had a unique way of getting to the heart of a situation without making the other person defensive.

John appreciated the opportunity to openly discuss his comments and feelings. "Kip, I've gone over and over the conversation in my mind these past several weeks. I believe I told the truth as I saw it, but it sure didn't come across that way."

"Maybe it was the truth, but I suspect that it was *your* truth," said Kip, smiling. "Sometimes our personal truths, beliefs, or convictions aren't someone else's, and that is generally where the trouble begins. As we try harder and harder to convince the other person, the effect is exactly the opposite of what we want.

"John, do you remember Peter and Alan's story? Well, I never told you what happened."

"I know," said John.

"These men had been close friends. They had admired each other. Now they loathed each other, and this had come about because of their communications, not because of their Shared Values."

"I know, but these things happen, don't they?" asked John, somewhat perplexed.

"Well John, I'll tell you now. During the drive to New Jersey, something magical happened. Alan confessed to Peter his anxieties and his part in causing the Cold War, and Peter did the same. Once they had shifted the conversation from a battle of styles and messages to admitting how they had each contributed to the situation, they began on the road to healing their partnership. Here were two guys weaving their way through Saturday traffic, working together for a common cause: landing an important account. It was a defining moment in their relationship."

John understood what Kip was offering him—an approach to patch things up.

"The breakthrough began after Alan realized what he was truly rooting for—to get to the meeting on time. This not only turned the day into a success, but started the transition from a no-win situation—involving enormous hurt feelings, deep anger, and frustration—into the beginning steps of rekindling the friendship between Peter and Alan. Alan turned to Peter and said, 'This is great. We're working together again. I guess we need to stop trying to convince each other of anything, and instead focus on the areas of interest we have in common and stop competing with each other.' Alan had stated the obvious, of course, but this breakthrough statement was the defining moment for the two men. By the time they reached the presentation site, their Berlin Wall was coming down."

"I'd bet even the client saw the difference," said John.

"I'm sure they did. It was this difference that turned their luck around. In fact, Peter and Alan received the nod to begin development of a three-million-dollar ad campaign. Not all stories have such a happy ending. Luckily, this one did.

"John, here were two men who had a lot in common. Their intentions were good, they each recognized the other's talents, but they forgot one very important thing: To respect another person's ideas and contributions requires extraordinary caring and commitment. The Heroic act of *putting the interests of others first* applies here. John, sometimes in our enthusiasm to convince, we say things that *diminish* the other person's *trust* in us.

"Further, we are ignoring the other person's need for *personal autonomy, significance,* and *acceptance.* And when we forget these needs, it leads to what you described as the other fellow's frustration, anger, and hurt feelings."

Kip wanted to make sure that his younger companion was receiving the information in the way in which it was intended. "John, how does this sync with what happened to you?"

John had listened intently to Kip's explanation. "I guess I wasn't acting Heroically, was I?"

"John, I can't say. But it sure seems like you should get a second chance. Remember that you said he wrote you a note? Well, from my experience, when a person takes time to write a note, he is quietly hoping for a future opportunity to mend the fence.

"Perhaps, with the passage of time, now is the right moment to try. I'd say that you might consider moderating your energy while trying to persuade another person to your position, and focus on the areas that you agree on. I believe that's good advice for us all. What do you think?"

John realized that he now had enough insight and information to try to repair the damage. After all, he liked and respected the other fellow, and he had looked forward to their becoming friends. Instead, he had forgotten some truths about how to treat another person. He was convinced that it was worth the effort and looked forward to extending the olive branch as soon as he got back to the office.

"Kip, thanks for listening. I really needed to sort that out before I called it a night."

"John, we all run into walls...myself included. What I hope you know is that people are rooting for you, and I know that deep down, you're pulling for them."

It had been a long day. John would sleep well.

Chapter Eight

The Mystery of Organizational Success

EIGHT

The Mystery of
Organizational Success

John woke up at 5:58 A.M., just two minutes before his alarm was set to go off. As he reached to intercept its ring, he saw Kip sitting on his bunk reading, already shaved and dressed.

"Good morning," John said, as he moved himself into a sitting position.

"Morning," replied Kip, smiling. "Did you sleep well?"

"Yes, I did, thanks. Did you?"

"I did, but I don't need quite as much sleep as I used to. I usually get up around 4:00 A.M. and take a walk. Sometimes I go back to bed, and sometimes I don't."

"I'm glad you're awake, Kip. I was thinking about our conversation all night, and I have some more questions before I can really understand the role the four Work Styles play in an organization. Give me a couple of minutes to wash up and get dressed."

Upon John's return, the two men began talking.

Kip started. "Let me continue our discussion about these four individual styles by saying that they are *all* necessary in a Heroic organization. For years, I enthusiastically searched for what I came to call *the mystery of organizational success.*"

"Why is it a mystery?" asked the younger man.

"Well John, because if the four Dominant Work Styles—the Hero, the Maverick, the 9-to-5-er, and the Dissident—aren't in place, you can't have a true Heroic Environment." Kip took a sheet of paper from his brief-case and drew a pie-shaped graph that showed how the four styles relate to each other.

"You see, only when an organization has all four personality types working as a unit will it reach its potential. These four styles act as a balanced system that allows an organization to recognize change and creatively respond to opportunities," Kip said with enthusiasm.

"I can understand needing the first three, but why would you want the Dissident Work Style?" asked John.

"Because, without occasional Dissident behavior, the organization is vulnerable and brittle. This inflexibility causes major blind spots, and a bout with disaster is only a matter of time," said the older man.

"A Hero who isn't occasionally challenged by a Dissident will lose his humility and blunder. A Maverick who isn't championed by a Hero will become frustrated. A 9-to-5-er who isn't inspired by a Hero will lose enthusiasm. Heroes and Mavericks who are not supported by 9-to-5-ers will lose time and effectiveness."

John realized the truth of what he was hearing. "It all works together so naturally, it seems. But suppose you have an organization that has an autocratic environment. What happens then?"

"Simply stated, organizations that are autocratic—those we've referred to as top-down Pyramids—tend to scare away the Heroes and Mavericks. That is why really talented and hard-working people fail in one organization and succeed in another." Kip then drew what an autocratic environment would look like.

"See, in essence, 9-to-5-ers and Dissidents are running the ship. Now, both 9-to-5-ers and Dissidents are important, but they can't carry the full load without help. Help comes in the form of Heroes, and Heroes facilitate the Mavericks, who generate ideas and instigate conversations."

"So, Heroes and Mavericks are the most important types," said John.

"No, all four styles are important. The key is balance," said Kip.

"Well, is there ever a time when you can't find Heroes and Mavericks, even when the environment would be responsive to them?" asked John.

Kip replied, "Because everyone can be a Hero at the right moment, you don't have to worry about never having enough Heroes. By simply creating an environment that is Heroic, you will never have a shortage. The secret or mystery is in understanding the need for a balance of these four styles."

"I understand that a balance of the four Work Styles is necessary, but wouldn't it be better to get rid of all Dissidents?" asked John.

"Remember, all of us show Dissident behavior from time to time, especially when we're frustrated with things in the organization that are beyond our control. The Dissident's style keeps everyone honest. Dissidents are like investigative reporters. Their role is important because they challenge widely held beliefs that may be wrong. In fact, a Heroic Environment is a safe place for Dissidents to express their frustrations," added Kip.

Realizing they hadn't had breakfast yet, Kip suggested they get down to the dining car before it got too crowded.

"I agree. I'm starving!" said John.

As the two men walked to the dining car, John began to crystallize his understanding of why a balance of the four Dominant Work Styles was critical to the success and survival of his organization.

Chapter Nine

The Curse of Conditional Thinking

NINE

The Curse of
Conditional Thinking

The morning sun broke cleanly through the high clouds as the train sped toward its next stop. Some passengers would be leaving the train, but John still had a long way to go, not in miles but in understanding. He knew that he would have Kip's company for only a little while longer, and he wanted to make every minute count.

As they entered the dining car, John turned and said, "Kip, sometimes I just wish the people around me would change."

"What do you mean, *change?*" asked Kip, as he glided into his window seat.

"What I really mean to say is that some of the things people say or do get me downright angry and frustrated!"

"And what do you generally do about it?" asked Kip, looking John straight in the eye.

"I get angry and stew about it mostly," John replied. "You know, sometimes I think my emotions get in the way of thinking clearly at such a moment. Is that hard to understand?"

"Not at all, John. Frankly, it took me quite a few years to understand that emotions often block our most productive thoughts. And they sometimes even put us on the wrong trail in terms of finding solutions to our interpersonal dilemmas. Let me see if I can explain what I mean.

"All of us, as we mature, begin to develop a sense of what's okay and what's *not* okay. Think of it this way: Unknowingly, we begin to develop a gigantic set of lists. Now, these lists identify *everything* we do and everything everyone else does. Not only do we develop our own lists, but we are careful to make sure that our internal rating system values every item on the list.

"Because it's our list and our rating system, we are pretty sure of being right about our opinions and impressions. I bet you've heard the expression, 'That's what makes a horse race.'"

John looked puzzled. "No, I haven't. What does it mean?"

"Well, when I was a young man, I couldn't understand why some people wore one type of hat and other people wore different hats. When I asked my mother, she said, 'That's what makes a horse race.'

"She was suggesting that if everyone wore the same hat, or bet on the same horse, it would be a pretty dull world. John, people see the world differently, and that's the beauty of it all. And that's one of the greatest strengths of any operation—its diversity. There's no way we are all going to vote for the same candidate or practice the same religion. People innately want to be able to choose. The French say, 'Vive la difference!'

"But the truth is, even though people see things differently, we don't usually give them credit for their choices, especially if their choices seem strange or out of step with our idea of how things should be. Unless we take control and are more forgiving, our rating system starts to get us in trouble. Left unchecked, it could lead us to become narrow-minded, or worse."

John could now see Kip's point. He was gently suggesting that John's rating system was getting in the way of giving other people their rightful places in the spotlight and allowing them to be different. John's frustration and impatience with other people's behavior were leading him to judge people according to his standards of how the world was "supposed" to be.

"I never thought of having an internal rating system, but now that you bring it up, I do have standards and beliefs. Maybe I do judge others by my standards, but what's so wrong with that?" asked John. "Doesn't everyone?"

"Of course they do," said Kip emphatically, "and that's what starts to cause some pretty interesting dilemmas. Not only do we have an internal rating system, but so does everyone else. That, of course, is what happened between our friends Peter and Alan.

"And to complicate this, we each compare our rating system to others. Each rating system gets modified somewhat when we realize that we need to compare notes—then we have a chance to sort out our differences."

"I know it's better to get your differences out in the open, but I don't always do that," said John.

"John, give yourself some slack. Believe me, no one ever does all the time either. But when we don't discuss our differences, we begin to go down the path of what I call *conditional thinking.*"

"What the heck is conditional thinking?" asked John.

"Conditional thinking occurs when we place conditions of acceptance and support on those around us. Let me explain by giving you an example.

"Let's say that you're working with someone over an extended period of time, and you begin to notice his or her X's and O's more strongly than you did when you first met this person. X's and O's are the pluses and minuses that we all have. Over time, we begin to learn about people we work with, and their X's and O's start to show up in living color. John, everyone has them. Even me, I'm sorry to say. If we began to work with each other day-in and day-out, we'd learn plenty about each other."

"Yeah, and you'd learn about my O's pretty darned fast!" said John, smiling.

"Well, John, it isn't the fact that you have your faults that matters—it's how the rest of us think about your faults that really counts," said Kip. "During my many years of working with people, I've come to understand a critical approach.

"We begin to justify in our own minds why we can no longer unconditionally support the other person. But because we need to continue to work with them, we begin to *conditionally* support them. You'll always know that conditional support is occurring when you hear people say, 'I can't support you 100 percent on that; I must take exception to this or that.'"

"What's so bad about that approach?" asked John.

"Just about everything!" said Kip. "When we start to put conditions on our support of other people, we are destroying the thing that binds us together: our *trust* in each other. Sure, we can have disagreements; that's normal. But our disagreements should not destroy our support for one another. "

"Here are some examples of how dangerous conditional support and conditional thinking are. Imagine if in international politics we heard, *'I can only support the treaty and my defense commitments 70 percent of the time.'* Or in a marriage, if one partner said, *'I'm only faithful 80 percent of the time.'*

"How about in living by a labor contract? *'I adhere to the contract 90 percent of the time.'* In driving a car? *'I abide by the rules of the road 70 percent of the time.'*

"John, you can see how dangerous this conditional approach can be. And, oh yes, people who conditionally support are *never* really satisfied. The moment one condition is met, something comes up that sets off their discontent all over again."

"Gee, Kip, I never looked at it that way. But what's the alternative?"

"John, I'm glad you asked. The easiest way to answer your question is to ask you a question in return. If you were to live your life devoid of conditional thinking, how would you do it?"

"That's simple," said John. "I'd give people my full support! And I wouldn't place conditions on my commitments to them."

"Bravo, John!" said Kip. "It really is as simple as that. And you will know that you've gotten rid of conditional thinking when the snide comments, backdoor conversations, second-guessing, and critical expressions start disappearing from *your* behavior. And when this happens, our personal internal lists and rating systems of what's acceptable and what's not also disappear."

John had a puzzled look on his face. "But what about all the differences I have with other people? You know, some of the people I work with are pretty frustrating."

"John, the best advice I can give you is to throw away your forms and checklists and start talking out your differences. Here are five quick guidelines for building an approach to remove conditional thinking from your life:

"**Number one**, approach the other person about the issue you have with them within twenty-four hours. We call it the 'Twenty-Four Hour Rule.'

"**Number two**, ask the other person if this a good time to communicate. In fact, I suggest you always use the same phrase, 'Is this a good time to talk?' And then wait for a response. Make sure that if the other person says it's not a good time to talk, you schedule a better time before you leave. We call this rule the Joan-Rivers rule. You know the famous comedian whose monologue started with that phrase?"

"Yeah, I know, 'Can We Talk?' " Both men smiled. "What's rule number three?"

"**Number three** is to make sure you approach the other person in a nonthreatening way. Only the other person can truly determine whether you're successful with this one. It will take practice to be able to read his or her reaction and tell when you're coming across in a threatening manner.

"**Number four**, when you have your conversation with the other person, be straightforward without hurting the other person's feelings. Keep your language simple, understandable, and above all, nonapologetic and nonpersonal. And finally…

"**Number five**, make sure that you make requests of the other person and don't give him or her complaints or opinions. I'd also go one step further and tell the other person how you'd like things to be. Don't demand anything—just make a straightforward, respectful request. And that's the key to all this—making fair requests.

John was writing on his napkin as fast as he could. "Kip, these five guidelines seem as though they could be used at home as well as at work."

"You bet they can. In fact, I'd teach them to everyone. After all, if they work for you, they should—and do—work for everyone, even our kids."

"They also seem like a set of standards. Are they the standards for any of the eight Heroic Principles?"

"So, you picked up on that, did you? Yes John, these five steps are the standards for *treating others with uncompromising truth*. How do you like these guidelines?"

"I love them. In fact, if I understand you correctly, I can use these guidelines to rid myself of conditional thinking and to make a real change in the way I communicate with my coworkers to make my thoughts and feelings known."

Kip was pleased with John's response. "Now, I caution you to make sure that your differences are fundamental to moving your organization forward and do not stem from your personal ideas of how things should be. Remember, we all have our own style of doing things. Some of us are pretty private by nature, others talk in a slow and deliberate way, some of us look at a situation from every angle, and others are enthusiastic and emoting.

"Some of us," Kip continued, "like to wear our hair long, while others like to wear their hair short. All personality types, like our Heroes, Mavericks, 9-to-5-ers, and Dissidents, are found in every organization and must be respected and defended for their differences and their personal expressions. These differences are at the very heart of every team's strength. Again, it's all about diversity and inclusion. Cut out or shun one of these personalities, and your organization will not have the depth necessary to grow and change rapidly.

"And John, one more thing. I believe that politicking your point of view is always destructive and counterproductive in the final analysis. Talking with another individual to shore up your collective values and shared goals is important and fundamental in sustaining a long-lasting relationship. But seeking group support for your ideas or point of view before you go to the person you are in conflict with causes future misunderstandings and adds to the negative political nature of an organization. Not only does it undermine the other person's trust in you, but it does nothing for your credibility. Remember, to everyone else you come across as someone who may also be talking about them.

"George Washington said, 'One man makes a majority.' Be confident in your judgment. It takes practice, but it's worth taking the risk for the organization's sake. Stop going around testing the water to see if others agree with your point of view."

In a few short moments, John had gained invaluable insight into how to be free from the trap of *conditional thinking*. It was a lesson that he would need to practice when he got home to Denver, and he was eager to begin.

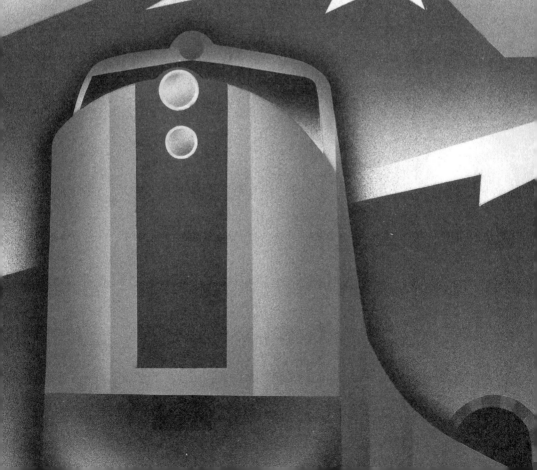

Chapter Ten

The Role of the Navigator in a Heroic Environment

TEN

The Role of the Navigator in a Heroic Environment

As soon as they were back in Compartment 417-C, John looked at Kip thoughtfully. John was excited about the morning's breakfast conversation because he could use Kip's guidelines with his family as well as his coworkers. He loved his wife very much and could see how his conditional thinking was eroding their relationship. Even his thoughts about his daughter, Lauren, were colored by his conditional thinking. He knew he would be seeing his family in less than two hours, and he could hardly wait.

With the information Kip had given him, John knew he could now make intelligent, thoughtful decisions about his career and readjust his approach to the people he loved or worked with. He was armed with important insights into how people really wanted to be treated.

While Kip arranged his papers, John asked, "Kip, before our journey together ends, are there any other important areas we should cover?"

"Well, let me see. Hmmm...let's talk about change," said Kip. "Perhaps one of the most important things to understand is the tremendous speed at which change occurs today. This is especially true in business, where economic conditions, technological breakthroughs, and consumer preferences can unearth new opportunities or cause a loss of business almost overnight.

"The problem is that most organizations aren't set up to respond quickly enough to change."

"I'm sure you're right," said John, "but there are a lot of old-style, autocratic companies that keep making a profit year after year. It's hard to argue for a change when their stock prices keep going up."

"You might think there are a lot of old companies out there, but that's not really the case," said Kip. "Here are some statistics which might interest you. By 1970, more than half of the Fortune 500 companies of 1955 were eaten up by mergers or closed for lack of profitability. By the middle of the 1980s, few of the 1955 Fortune 500 companies remained in business under their original names or with the descendants of their original management groups. Imagine, only 71 survived.

"By the turn of the twentieth century, entire manufacturing and service industries had been reinvented. At least half of the people who had a particular job in 2004 will have a new one requiring new skills by 2010. Companies that will lead every nation's economy are forming as we speak, and the ones we currently know may not make it through the transition. There are no lifetime job guarantees anymore, even for model workers and managers. Everyone is facing change!"

"What can we do to prepare for this?" asked John.

"There are many things we can do. The wrong response is to put our heads in the sand. In the short-term, that might work, but it's not a great solution long-term." Kip's eyes twinkled in amusement.

Getting serious again, Kip continued. "The common thread among the organizations in the most danger is that they don't have a strategy or a culture that adapts quickly to change.

"John, the reason most companies disappear is that they lack the process to accept and benefit from new information and to make the appropriate course corrections. If you think any company is immune from this disease, you're wrong. Even the biggest or 'bluest' aren't immune."

John knew exactly which organizations Kip was singling out.

"Even government and the educational system in our country need to heed this warning," Kip said. "Nothing is forever. Any organization that forgets its job is to serve customers and to meet their ever-changing needs is a target for extinction. Once an organization loses sight of this fact, it's headed for the scrap heap. Just look at the coal and rail industries; at one time they thought they were immune to change. I think the oil industry and the internal-combustion engine are next.

"John, without the ability to see the future, organizations tragically lose their way. In most instances, a safe passage is not clearly marked, and it requires sharp navigators and able communicators to find the way."

"I bet you're going to say that each company that is to survive listens to its employees and is able to effectively interpret its Business and People Values. How do you define a Navigator?" asked John.

"*Navigators* are the people who have a vision of the organization's future and help navigate toward it. Navigators are crucial to organizations because they are alert to the danger signals and convey advance information to the rest of the organization. They help the organization heed the warnings and make appropriate choices."

"Isn't it the role of management to anticipate change?" asked John.

"In the old days, we expected top management to have all the vision. But in a Heroic Environment, the Navigators *are not just the senior managers* in the organization; they're on the frontlines, too. In a Heroic Environment, we need everyone's help to see the future.

"No longer will tradition or rank forecast our future. Past reputations, successes, and even learned lessons will not be enough to survive and prosper. A new partnership must be developed between management and the employees of an organization. You might consider it a new communication and philosophical contract between the two groups. Remember, we spoke of TransAction Points; well this idea now becomes even more important.

"Here is a chart one of my friends put together of the new relationship between Front-Line Workers, Wise Counsels, and top management on the roles and expectations of each group in the TransAction Zone. See what you think.

ROLES AND EXPECTATIONS IN THE TRANSACTION ZONE™

Front Line Workers	Wise Counsels	Top Managers
MAKE GREAT CUSTOMER TRANSACTIONS *Remove TransAction Blocks and make Great Customer TransActions*	**PARTNER WITH FRONT-LINE WORKERS** *Help staff remove TransAction Blocks and make Great Customer TransActions*	**CREATE A GREAT CUSTOMER TRANSAC-TION ENVIRONMENT** *Challenge the staff to question anything that impedes Great Customer TransActions*
1. **Communicate what's going on** in the TransAction Zone and at the TransAction Point	1. **Coach**—help others learn and grow regardless of their roles	1. **Be a Visionary Leader**—help everyone understand the organization's purpose
2. **Measure the system's capacity** to deliver Great Customer TransActions and suggest improvements	2. **Counsel**—help others discover their own answers without imposing your answers or judgments	2. **Encourage everyone to develop a Keen Internal Vision**—a personal vision that supports the organization's purpose
3. **Work independently**, as much as possible, to deliver Great Customer TransActions and to remove TransAction Blocks	3. **Provide and Locate Resources**—provide staff with the time, manpower, money, and other resources they need to deliver Great Customer TransActions	3. **Champion a Shared Values® Heroic Environment®**—that supports Great Customer TransActions
4. **Work together with others**, when the situation requires it, to deliver Great Customer TransActions and to remove TransAction Blocks	4. **Be a Financial and TransAction Steward**—help everyone understand their part in protecting the financial health of the organization	4. **Create a Safe Environment**—where the staff is eager to find a solution to every TransAction Block
5. **Challenge any system**, policy, process, or work-flow that inhibits Great Customer TransActions	5. **Be a Visionary Leader**—help everyone understand how their work supports the organization's purpose	5. **Promote Great Customer TransActions**—by challenging the staff to build flexibility into the organization's policies, processes, systems, and workflows

"In the future, organizations that ignore this vital partnership between the Front-Line Worker and management will fail. Maintaining old, autocratic, controlling tactics and *centralizing strategies* will become a noose around many organizations' throats. 'Fast and lean' will become the order of the day. Right now, organizations are consolidating and merging, but in the future the advantage will go to those companies who choose to share responsibility and vital market and financial information with their people. If an organization wants to know about its Achilles' heel, it needs to address the phenomenon which I call *filtered information!*"

"What do you mean, 'filtered information'?" asked John.

"Filtered information is information that has been screened before it's sent upstairs. Think of it this way: Let's suppose you saw a trend that you felt could adversely affect the future of the company, but you also knew that this information went against the beliefs of the CEO and, more than likely, would be immediately rejected and could even put your career at risk. Would you send it upstairs?" asked Kip.

"Probably not, but if I did, I would at least word it so that it and I might have a chance to survive in an autocratic environment," said John.

Kip immediately jumped on his words. "Exactly, then you'd be sending filtered information upstairs, instead of sending the strong medicine needed for your senior managers to assess the situation correctly and make the necessary changes.

"Keep in mind, your leaders believe they are receiving fresh, unscreened information, not filtered information. They believe with certainty that they are considering the most current data. If they are using filtered information, their basis will be wrong and their decisions will be wrong!

"Autocratic environments that view the very existence of contrary and dissenting information as threatening and destabilizing are brittle and unable to affect change quickly, if at all. And because these organizations create a culture that is threatening to people, the only information they receive is filtered. In chain-of-command environments, it's amazing that *any* information is unfiltered. As a result, they lose the competitive edge they need to survive. And they don't even understand the true cause of their vulnerability."

"Don't they recognize the danger of receiving filtered information and facilitating poor communications?" asked John.

"Yes, of course they would recognize the danger, if they realized the incoming information was screened. But because they expect to see continuously confirming data, and not contradictory data, they feel comfortable," said the older man.

"I think I know what you are getting at," said John. "They don't receive a different point of view, and so they believe they're on the right track. And if someone has a different view, they say, 'He doesn't seem to have the right style.'"

"Yes, John. You know, in modern organizations, we don't burn witches. We simply don't keep people around who see things differently." Kip continued. "Organizational discipline is the glue that holds autocratic and controlling businesses together. Their leaders' powers are tied up in their belief systems of, often, an outdated vision. These strong beliefs create a thick stone wall and unknowingly filter out vital information about changing market forces."

"I understand the wisdom of sharing unfiltered information," said John. "People at all levels of an organization have good ideas that must be heard, even if the information is unpopular. But what is management's new leadership role?"

Kip responded. "Management's most important role in the change process is to create an environment that openly challenges all its sacred cows. Unfortunately, management in the Pyramid thinks its role is to *anticipate* change. You cannot plan to see change; if it were that simple, everyone would institute such a policy. Yet, when management selects a small group of senior people, including themselves, to take on this task to anticipate change, they usually fail."

"I would never have believed management's role is to encourage challenging the sacred cows. I've always believed top management's job was to see the future," said John.

At that, Kip asked John for the TransAction Zone graphic so he could make another point regarding its importance. John placed the graphic on the compartment's table for them both to look at.

TransAction Zone™ Design
Focus On Making The TransAction

The customer drives the TransAction.
Each customer has a group to support their product and service needs. The organization's size dictates the number of TranAction Zones.

Kip smiled. "Management's ultimate role is to create the *conditions* for others to see and respond to change and to take advantage of opportunities. That's why this new design is so important. It's management's role to encourage Navigators to show the organization the way. I'm not suggesting that management take a passive position, but their emphasis should be to encourage full participation at every level, including the Front-Line Worker.

"In fact, it should be considered imperative for management to promote full participation at every level—especially on the front-lines. They must encourage everything and anything to be challenged that impedes delivering services and products to internal and external customers. I call this approach the establishment of a 'new citizenship' within an organization," Kip said. "In a Heroic Environment, it's essential that everyone be involved in not only defining problems, but also finding solutions. You see, you and I and every other human being share something called *perceptual bias.*"

"Wait a minute," said John. "You just threw a ten-dollar word at me!"

Kip smiled. "I'm sorry. Let me explain. Perceptual bias occurs when people see what they expect to see and ignore what they don't expect to see—or don't want to see."

"You mean like not seeing your car keys that are right under your nose?" asked John.

"That's it exactly, but sometimes the consequences are a lot more dramatic," said Kip. "Perceptual biases are frightening because we don't know we have them. They're *invisible* to us, but their effects are not! Management's best strategy is to create a responsive environment that encourages employees to come up with innovative approaches to solving problems, rather than trying to see all the changes themselves and to be open to lots of experimenting. Frankly, John, there are lots of ways to do things. And so we should leave the 'doing decisions' up to the Front-Line Workers. With this philosophy, senior managers reduce stress on themselves and remain responsible for the overall results—the creation of a culture that learns, adapts, and innovates on the fly instead of following outdated rules.

"The combination of self-management and personal responsibility provides the best opportunity for an organization to see change and respond to changing world markets and international competition. Again, these two elements must reside in the same person—the Front-Line Worker. John, think of it as *upward coaching,* the power to look, hear, and act at the baseline of the organization, and push unfiltered information to every part of the operation.

"I'm not a fortune teller, but I'll bet that soon we'll see more and more good news business stories in every industry about companies that are taking this approach. Those businesses that share the 'company keys' with their employees will see dramatic results!" said Kip. "I call this kind of openness with staff *'Adventuring* with your people.' It's the new way to lead. As more and more organizations move in this direction, remaining a top-down Pyramid will be the kiss of death."

"That's quite a prediction!" remarked John. "I guess President Harry Truman said it best: 'If you can't stand the heat, get out of the kitchen.' But I think I like the kitchen, especially if it's in a Heroic Environment." The two men grinned.

Kip continued. "I'm afraid the alternative to this approach is going out of business."

John looked over his notes of what Kip had shared up to this point. "Let me see if I can summarize what you've been telling me, Kip:

- "Heroic Environments create a bond by which all people within an organization participate fully in its shared purpose, and they do this by creating a common language of values and standards.

- "A company can ensure its survival and success by understanding that market forces will continue to change and that it is up to the Navigators—at all levels of the organization—to make sure that *unfiltered* information continues to be communicated upstairs as well as downstairs, no matter how difficult it is to hear.

- "With the right environment in place, companies are able to take advantage of new ideas that will spontaneously spring from any and all corners."

"You're really catching on," said Kip. "Wise managers know that all employees need to become *insiders* within their organization in order to help manage the challenging activity of seeing change."

After a slight pause, Kip continued. "Organizations that understand the importance of receiving unfiltered information, encouraging different opinions, applauding fresh approaches, and continuing to look for the important content without being blinded by the style of its delivery will prosper far into the twenty-first century."

"I think I now understand what you mean about needing Navigators at *all* levels within an organization," said John. "I guess you could say that *everybody* within an organization needs to put on the hat of the Navigator."

The morning skyline of Denver was now just a few bends in the tracks ahead. Though this trip was ending, John's journey of discovery was just beginning.

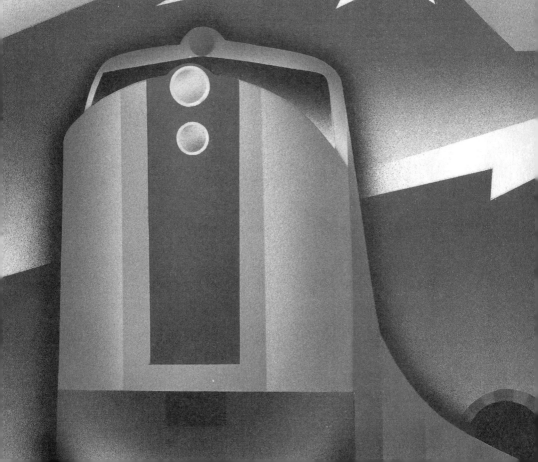

The Importance of Having a Tracking Motor

The Importance of Having a Tracking Motor

K ip broke in with an additional thought about the role of the Navigator. "I'd like to help you understand how impor- tant this concept of navigation is by telling you a story."

Kip was about to explain the reason why organizations lose their way and disappear and why organizations that were once powerful beyond imagination have found themselves on the scrap heap of business history. More importantly, he was about to give John the formula for an organization's long-term survival.

Kip began. "A fellow I know was traveling the United States representing a good-sized company. In a hotel in one of the cities he frequented was a shop with a telescope in the display window. He had always been intrigued by telescopes but had never owned one, so he decided to take the opportunity that day to learn more about them. It wasn't until years later that he realized what he had learned about telescopes that day was an important lesson that applied to business."

"Could that fellow have been you?" asked John, with a smile.

Kip returned John's smile, but didn't respond to his question. Instead he went on, "The store clerk's hobby was astronomy. He knew a great deal about telescopes, including the importance of using a tracking motor."

"What's a tracking motor?" asked John.

"A tracking motor is used to photograph stars and constellations," explained Kip. "The salesman showed the fellow two photographs. In the first photo, the stars appeared blurry, faded and streaked.

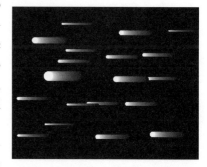

In the second, they were crystal clear. The first photo was taken without a tracking motor, the second with a tracking motor running. What the tracking motor does is 'track' the stars as they move across they sky. You see, to the naked eye, stars appear to be stationary; but with a telescope, the movement of the stars becomes apparent. A tracking motor compensates for this movement and keeps the photograph in focus."

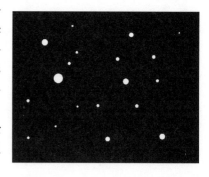

"So what's a tracking motor got to do with business?" asked John.

"Let me explain. In order for a business to survive, it needs to be able to 'track' the rapid movement of market forces. Those that don't won't survive," Kip replied.

"I see!" said John. "That graphic you showed me earlier from *The Economist* illustrates your point perfectly. Organizations are becoming less and less profitable because they are failing to 'track' rapidly-changing market forces."

"Precisely!" replied Kip. "They make market observations from a *static* point of view. Too often, they assume that present market conditions will continue unchanging into the future. And when their market share and sales begin to slip, they slash prices, quality and service, and as a result, their profits slip even further.

"This static point of view would explain why, in the 1950s, Ford Motor Company rejected Toyota's request to help market their trucks. Ford believed that Americans wouldn't buy Japanese trucks or cars. This would also explain why Western Union looked at the telephone and rejected it as impractical, and it would explain why Hewlett-Packard turned down Steve Jobs' idea of marketing the personal computer."

"I can think of dozens of other companies that have fallen into the same trap," commented John.

"There are hundreds, if not thousands, of companies that have fallen victim to *static observation* of market forces," replied Kip. "They've switched off their market 'tracking motor.' For some reason, as successful companies mature, their own success leads them to believe they will always be successful following the same formula that made them successful in the first place. By the time leadership realizes that they are no longer tracking the market, it's often too late and their organizations are headed for the rocks."

"I'm afraid I may be working for one of those companies!" said John.

"Many of us have and are," replied Kip.

"Can the market tracking motor be switched back on before it's too late?"

"Yes of course it can," Kip reassured. "But an organization has to recognize that they've lost track of the market and take steps to get their tracking motor running again."

"What steps?" asked John.

"Glad you asked!" replied Kip.

Chapter Twelve

Restarting & Sustaining Your Tracking Motor

Restarting & Sustaining Your Tracking Motor

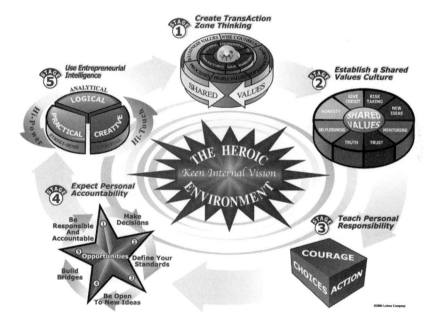

The Five Stages for Creating and Sustaining *The Heroic Environment*

"When I was learning to hit a baseball, my dad would tell me to keep my eye on the ball. That is also a key lesson in keeping an operation's tracking motor on. With rapidly-moving market forces, keeping your eye on the 'ball' of market forces is the key to creating the Heroic Environment. And, when you have your tracking motor on, each individual has a sense of his or her *Keen Internal Vision.*

"There are five steps, or stages, a company must go through to restart its tracking motor in order to create and sustain the *Heroic Environment.*"

Stage 1: Create TransAction Zone Thinking

"The first stage is to *Create TransAction Zone Thinking.* TransAction Zone Thinking recognizes the importance of letting the *customer's* needs or requests, rather than the company's policies and processes, drive the TransAction. TransAction Zone Thinking places Front-Line Workers in a one-on-one relationship with their customers at the *TransAction Point.* All of the organization's functions,

Create TransAction Zone Thinking

STAGE 1

systems and values are arranged to support transActions that are seen by both the customer and the Front-Line Worker as a gift."

John interrupted, "I get it; the goal is to make each customer transAction a present."

"Exactly! By designing relationships with both our internal and external customers in this way, the Front-Line Worker's ability to provide each unique customer with what they want and need improves dramatically. TransAction Zone Thinking says to Front-Line Workers, 'Use your best judgment to satisfy your customer. The responsibility for delivering what the customer wants is entirely yours.' If you run into any problems, it's your responsibility not to throw your hands up and say 'the systems or my boss won't let me,' but to identify the TransAction Block and either remove it yourself or ask for assistance from your coworkers or Wise Counsel."

"Wow!" said John. "I'd love to have that kind of freedom and flexibility in dealing with my customers. But my company would need the kind of culture that would support TransAction Zone Thinking."

"Good point, John! That leads me the second stage in turning your 'Tracking Motor' on."

Establish a Shared Values Culture
STAGE 2

Stage 2: Establish a Shared Values Culture

"Stage Two is *Establish a Shared Values Culture*. We've already discussed the power of the eight Shared Values at length, John. But if I were to sum up a Shared Values Culture using one value, it would be *'putting the interests of others before our own.'* That's what TransAction Zone Thinking is all about, putting the interests of our customers first. After all, if we don't satisfy the needs of our customers, they will go elsewhere and our organization will cease to exist."

"I agree, customers should be the reason for our organization's existence. So, what's stage three?" asked John eagerly.

Teach Personal Responsibility

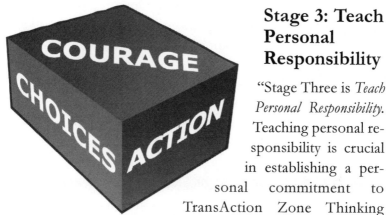

Stage 3: Teach Personal Responsibility

"Stage Three is *Teach Personal Responsibility.* Teaching personal responsibility is crucial in establishing a personal commitment to TransAction Zone Thinking from everyone in the operation. There can be no exceptions. Teaching personal responsibility may take longer than you'd like, but once people become personally responsible, the organization can move mountains. A 'Can-Do' attitude becomes infectious. There are **Three Elements of Personal Responsibility:**

"First, individuals must be given the responsibility of making *choices,* of making decisions without asking permission or being second-guessed. That's what 'using your best judgment' is all about. But teaching individuals to make choices cannot be imposed from the top; learning to make choices must initially be voluntary until they've developed enough courage.

"Which brings me to the second element, developing *courage.* Make no mistake, taking responsibility is not easy; it takes courage.

Helping Front-Line Workers to develop courage is something that takes time and patience—time to learn how to take on more responsibility, and patience to develop confidence in yourself. But if the organization continues to play the 'blame game,' punishing people for making mistakes and using performance reviews or appraisal systems that stress conformity, expecting people to display courage is unrealistic.

"The third element is *action.* Agreeing to take on new responsibilities means nothing until you take action at the TransAction Point to satisfy the customer's needs. If mistakes are made, we fix the mistakes, learn from them and move on. The real opportunity is to continue to gain knowledge and understanding of 'how the work works.'

"The underlying premise in a Heroic Environment is that people don't get up in the morning intending to fail. So by focusing on the way we do business instead of personal mistakes, action will be taken, courage exhibited, and choices made."

"Kip, my company is always asking us to take on more responsibility. It's not that I'm unwilling. In fact, I'd love to have more responsibility, if only they'd stop checking on me every step of the way. I really resent being given responsibility and then having my supervisor constantly check on my progress and second-guess my decisions. And what really burns me up is that once I've finished a project, it's my supervisor who reports on my results and he often gets the credit!"

"I understand your frustration," Kip commiserated. "Let me explain why that happens by talking about stage four."

Stage 4: Expect Personal Accountability

"You see John, one of the fundamental problems in control-based organizations is that they *deliberately separate responsibility from accountability.* That's why you feel so frustrated.

Expect Personal Accountability

Responsibilities are delegated or assigned to you but the accountability remains with your supervisor. That's how control-based systems are designed, so don't blame your supervisor for checking on your progress, because it's his neck on the line! The control-based system has the entire responsibility and accountability dynamic upside down. Most of us have been brought up to believe that this separation is natural and so we never even challenge it.

"Think of it as institutionalizing the *parent–child* relationship. Let me illustrate. One of the greatest struggles we have with our teenagers is getting them to be accountable. As parents we push them to take on more and more responsibility as they mature, but they resist being accountable for their choices. Breaking out of the classic parent–child relationship is a real test for us as parents and for them as young adults. It's easy to regress to our old ways because they are so ingrained in our upbringing.

"That makes sense, Kip. So what's the solution?"

"The solution is to *Expect Personal Accountability* from everyone in the organization, from the CEO to the least-experienced Front-Line Worker. There are five opportunities that every staff member can enjoy in taking hold of the idea of personal accountability:

1. *Make decisions* that make sense for the customer, individual, and organization.

2. Take a moment and *define one's personal standards* of behavior, service, and quality.

3. *Be open to new ideas* and let go of old outdated ways of thinking that no longer serve the customer, individual, or organization.

4. *Build bridges and connections* to strengthen the service and quality levels within the organization. Build allies in this quest for more excellence.

5. *Be personally responsible and accountable for removing TransAction Blocks* that are getting in the way of *Creating Great Customer TransActions.*

And all my experience in introducing this new idea into organizations that wish to transform into a Heroic Environment suggests that people at every level are not only open to, but want this kind of responsibility and accountability. Now let's look at the final stage."

Stage 5: Use Entrepreneurial Intelligence

"Of course you know what an entrepreneur is: someone who sets up and finances new commercial enterprises with his or her own money. But the meaning really goes beyond Webster's definition. The spirit of entrepreneurship can be seen from the kid on the corner who sets up a lemonade stand to the United Nations' creation of UNICEF. Entrepreneurship, John, is a state of mind. *Entrepreneurial Intelligence* is the engine that makes or breaks any enterprise, whether it's a start-up company or it is celebrating its 100-year anniversary. Entrepreneurial Intelligence is made up of three inter-related dimensions:

1. **"Logical Intelligence.** *Logical intelligence* is that part of a person's and an organization's thinking that helps us *analyze* problems. It's the type of intelligence that we used most as we moved through school, where our teachers defined the problems, defined the solutions and then tested us on our ability to come up with the right answers. Unfortunately, in the real world, problems and solutions are not pre-defined for us. This requires two other kinds of intelligence: *Creative Intelligence and Practical Intelligence.*

2. **"Creative Intelligence.** *Creative Intelligence* helps us both identify problems and find solutions that have not been predefined for us. Creative Intelligence is more *spiritual* in nature than Logical Intelligence. That is, it connects our mind, spirit and temperament to the universe. Because Creative Intelligence is a spiritual idea, it is difficult to measure or predict, but it is absolutely necessary for personal and organizational success.

3. **"Practical Intelligence.** *Practical Intelligence* is that part of our intelligence that finds a way to make things work. We say that people with Practical Intelligence have *street sense* or just plain *common sense*. People and organizations with Practical Intelligence find a way to make things work."

"The concept of *Entrepreneurial Intelligence* is new for me," said John. "Could you elaborate a bit more?"

"Sure!" said Kip. "Let me explain how these three elements interact. First, no individual or organization is equally strong in all three elements. Yet, to be Entrepreneurially Intelligent, it's absolutely essential that we strike some semblance of *balance*. In doing so, we achieve a measure of both **Hi-Touch** and **Hi-Power.**"

"I'm not sure I follow," said John quizzically.

"Let me explain," said Kip. "Hi-Touch occurs when we combine logical and creative intelligence. It's more of a feminine trait, in that women seem to generally be more attuned to relationships than men. The point is that in combining the analytical and spiritual elements of thinking, we become more in tune with the needs of others and more able to find ways to strengthen relationships.

"Hi-Power occurs when we combine logical and practical intelligence. It's a more masculine trait, in that men generally seem to be more attuned to focusing on practical solutions. Combining analytical thinking with street-sense moves people and organizations toward finding workable solutions, whether or not they enhance relationships."

"The concept is starting to make more sense. Could you give me an example?" asked John.

"Sure," said Kip. "Many years ago, a man who hadn't even graduated from high school started a business. It wasn't a fancy business. In fact, it started off as nothing more than a hot dog stand. But in time, both his business and his family grew.

"Every morning the man would get up and start his day by filling his wagon with the supplies he would need to serve his customers. He had a thriving business because he had recognized that his hot dogs brought joy and a break from the ordinary. He became famous by topping each hot dog with mouth-watering sauerkraut, relish, peppers and spices. Some called his creations an art form. Before long, he had several hot dog stands.

"Years passed. His son grew up and graduated from the local university. The father was very proud of his son and he encouraged the boy to go on to graduate school in business. Upon graduating from business school, the boy joined his father, who had started off with a single hot dog stand and now had built it into a city-wide institution.

"His son began to study the father's business and to use the concepts he had learned at graduate school. The young man, thinking that the father was giving away 'too much value' for the price of his hot dogs, suggested that he cut back on some of the ingredients. The son's idea was to measure and weigh all the added ingredients, from the sauerkraut to the peppers, and to find cheaper products to replace them and standardize the delivery.

"Before long, the love affair the business had enjoyed with its loyal customers became strained. The father went to the son and questioned the young man's approach. The son replied, 'Dad, you don't have the professional business education I have. For years you've been giving away too much to your customers and it's costing us money.'

"As the business continued to decline, the son's answer was to cut back even more. He reproached his father for his old ways of doing business. A once- thriving enterprise, established on the principle of giving the customer a great product at a great price, had been turned into a business run on formulas and measurements.

"In the end, the customers were driven away by an attitude of indifference that was expressed in an ordinary hot dog that customers could have purchased anywhere. The son's advanced business education taught him all the analytical tools for running a business, but he had not experienced the equally important aspects of creativity and common sense."

John shook his head and smiled sadly at Kip's story. He could see parallels to his own experience in the electrical parts business. Once they had started down the road of never-ending cycles of cost-cutting and systematizing, his company had become vulnerable to the competition.

Kip interrupted John's train-of-thought. "Please understand that the son was interested in protecting his father's hard work, so we can't really blame him. After all, he was doing what he had been taught, 'Look at the numbers, standardize the operation and minimize costs!' Yet as we know, this was too narrow a view and too simplistic in its approach."

"But the son's approach seems so logical," said John.

Kip nodded. "John, it wasn't wrong to want to look at the numbers or to want to reduce waste! But it wasn't that simple. Business is never only about logic, numbers and systems. There are two other elements—common sense and creativity—that must never be overlooked. When these three entrepreneurial elements get out of balance, or one or more is overlooked, that's when a business runs off the tracks.

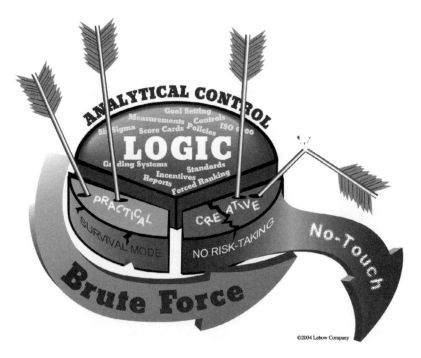

©2004 Lebow Company

"What I want to show you next is what someone drew up after one of my talks at a leading company interested in getting back on track. My subject that day was about why businesses lose their way. In the talk, I introduced the idea of staying in balance in order to stay in business and what happens when you don't."

Kip handed John a graphic that contrasted the Entrepreneurial chart with a distorted view of the Entrepreneurial Intelligence graphic. John took a long look at the graphic before addressing Kip.

"Kip, this graphic is interesting to me because it explains a lot about what has happened at my organization. We've been installing many of the programs listed in the 'logic' portion of the graphic."

"Independently, measurement and process improvement initiatives make sense," Kip said. "But taken to an extreme, they can overburden the workforce and overwhelm supervision.

"When an operation gets out of balance it will most certainly go out of business, and that's what we discussed with the Fortune 500 organizations that now number 71, down from the original 1955 list. But the causes of the impending demise of 429 companies were not apparent to the leadership of those organizations, and here's why. Leaders in those organizations read the numbers but rarely worked the line. They mistakenly thought managing meant *monitoring* instead of observing, first hand, the work, the processes, the machinery and the customers' reactions, both internally and externally.

"Had the young man in my story been required to work part of every week delivering hot dogs to customers, he would have heard their comments. But that's not what most managers do, and it's not what the young man did either. Talking to customers is a sure-fire way of finding out first-hand what is required to stay in business."

"Kip, I agree. Working on the front lines is essential to connecting with the pulse of the business and I think the last graphic describes it well."

"John, you're right on all points. You noted, I'm sure, that not only did logic dominate the balance of the three elements, but our essential need for Hi-Power and Hi-Touch was distorted even more. Hi-Power evolved into 'Brute Force,' and it overwhelmed Hi-Touch so that it became *No-Touch!*"

John now had the "big picture" and felt more confident about what he needed to do and what the pitfalls were. John knew he would need help from his coworkersto create the Heroic Environment Kip had outlined. Holding Kip's 5-stage chart in his hands gave John hope. He could hardly wait to get started.

Epilogue

The Beginning of a New Journey

EPILOGUE

The Beginning of a New Journey

Kip looked at his watch and said, "We'll be arriving in Denver in forty minutes." John didn't answer. He was torn between his great desire to see his family and his regret that he was about to say good-bye to his mentor.

Suddenly, he realized that he hadn't asked Kip enough questions about himself. In a way, it all seemed so mysterious. Yet, John felt a genuine sense of satisfaction about the mystery. It was as if the bond between them had been built purely around the nobility of the ideas they'd discussed.

Armed with these new concepts, John knew now that he would not change jobs. He would stay where he was and work to build a Heroic Environment.

After a long silence, John said, "Kip, I don't know how to thank you for all you've taught me."

Kip smiled. "You can thank me by letting me know how you're doing." And then, with special warmth, he added, "John, I think you know that I'm rooting for your success."

"Will you be coming through Denver on one of your future trips?"

"Yes, I'll be passing through in April."

John's eyes lit up. "I'd be honored to have you stay with us."

"That's very kind of you," said Kip, smiling. The two men shook hands and exchanged business cards. Ten minutes later the train began to slow.

After receiving a loving homecoming greeting from Kathy and Lauren, John and his family hurried away from the platform. Suddenly, he heard his name called. As he turned around, he was surprised to see the president and one of the vice presidents of his company.

"Mr. Williams," he exclaimed with surprise, "what are you doing here?"

"We were in Denver for a meeting at your plant with our Japanese partners when this blasted snowstorm closed the airport, so the corporate jet is useless. I have to be in Los Angeles in two days, so this is the only alternative."

John smiled, "It's not such a bad alternative, Sir. It may take longer, but it's amazing the new perspective a train ride can give you. Oh, by the way, where are you sitting?"

The president looked at his ticket. "Compartment 417-C."

Suppressing a smile, John responded simply, "Sir, when you get back to corporate headquarters, I'd like to call you. I believe there'll be a lot for us to talk about."

The Personal
Work Style Assessment

The Personal Work Style Assessment™

The Personal Work Style Assessment™ provides a glimpse of the four work styles that are typically found in most workplaces. Once you've completed this assessment, it will help you understand how your work style contributes to the overall productivity of your department and organization.

This assessment is most useful as a snapshot of your present mix of behaviors. Depending on how you are currently experiencing your workplace, your behavior and perspective may change. Your scores may validate, surprise, or challenge your self-perception.

PERSONAL WORK STYLE ASSESSMENT™

TransAction Zone™

PERSONAL WORK STYLE ASSESSMENT

Directions: Think about yourself in your work environment. For each question, rank order your responses as follows: (Use each number only one time per question.)

1 = Least like me   3 = Somewhat like me
2 = Somewhat unlike me   4 = Most like me

Write the number (1, 2, 3, or 4) in the *white box*.

Example

		4	
			2
3			
	1		

Which of the following best describes your priority at work?

1. My priority is to finish my work by the end of the day.
2. My priority is on righting the wrongs done to me and to others.
3. My priority is on achieving results by working with others.
4. My priority is on pursuing ideas that interest me.

Make sure your total score for this group = 10

Which of the following best describes how you view others?

5. I tend to see the flaws in others.
6. I tend to see the good in others.
7. I tend not to think much about others.
8. I tend to do what it takes to get along with others.

Make sure your total score for this group = 10

Which of the following best describes how others view you?

9. Others would describe me as competent.
10. Others would describe me as seldom satisfied.
11. Others would describe me as independent.
12. Others would describe me as a team player.

Make sure your total score for this group = 10

Total the scores in each column, then continue on next page.

1

PERSONAL WORK STYLE ASSESSMENT

Which of the following best describes how you make decisions?

13. I prefer to involve others in decision-making.

14. I prefer to make decisions independently.

15. I prefer to avoid making decisions for which I may be blamed.

16. I prefer to let others decide.

Make sure your total score for this group = 10

Which of the following best describes how you deal with problems?

17. I look for creative solutions on my own.

18. I look for mutually beneficial solutions by involving others.

19. I look for management to find solutions to problems.

20. I look for the people who caused the problems.

Make sure your total score for this group = 10

Which of the following best describes how you view the future?

21. I view the future as likely to be a continuation of the present.

22. I view the future as full of interesting personal challenges.

23. I view the future as something over which I have little control.

24. I view the future as something that can be shaped by working with others.

Make sure your total score for this group = 10

Which of the following best describes how you view new employees?

25. I view new employees as potential competitors.

26. I view new employees as potentially reducing my work load.

27. I view new employees as a potential source of new ideas.

28. I view new employees as potentially valuable teammates.

Make sure your total score for this group = 10

Total the scores in each column, then continue on next page.

Which of the following best describes what motivates you on the job?	A	B	C	D
29. Job security and good pay are what motivate me.				
30. Hanging tough until I find something better motivates me.				
31. Challenging projects and wonderful teammates motivate me.				
32. Freedom and independence motivate me.				

Make sure your total score for this group = 10

Which of the following best describes your attitude toward authority?	A	B	C	D
33. I am wary of those in authority.				
34. Those in authority are there to be a resource and to support me.				
35. Those in authority can be either a help or hindrance.				
36. I depend on those in authority to take care of me.				

Make sure your total score for this group = 10

Which of the following best describe how you communicate?	A	B	C	D
37. I communicate with others only when I need their input.				
38. I communicate only with those few people I can really trust.				
39. I communicate with others frequently, seeking & giving input.				
40. I communicate with others as needed to get along.				

Make sure your total score for this group = 10

	A	B	C	D	
Total Score in Each Column, THIS PAGE					
Total Score in Each Column, FIRST PAGE					
Total Score in Each Column, SECOND PAGE					
*TOTAL SCORE, EACH COLUMN					= 100

* The sum of this row should equal 100 points.

My Personal Work Style Profile

Circle your score for each work style in each column below.

Intensity	A = Hero	B = Maverick	C = 9-to-5-er	D = Dissident	
HIGH	40	40	40	40	**Understanding Your Personal Work Style Scores**
	39	39	39	39	
	38	38	38	38	
	37	37	37	37	
	36	36	36	36	
	35	35	35	35	
	34	34	34	34	**What does a high score mean?**
	33	33	33	33	A high score means that you often
	32	32	32	32	use this style.
	31	31	31	31	
MEDIUM	30	30	30	30	
	29	29	29	29	
	28	28	28	28	
	27	27	27	27	
	26	26	26	26	
	25	25	25	25	
	24	24	24	24	**What does a medium score mean?**
	23	23	23	23	A medium score means that you
	22	22	22	22	sometimes use this style.
	21	21	21	21	
LOW	20	20	20	20	
	19	19	19	19	
	18	18	18	18	
	17	17	17	17	
	16	16	16	16	
	15	15	15	15	**What does a low score mean?**
	14	14	14	14	A low score means that you
	13	13	13	13	seldom use this style.
	12	12	12	12	
	11	11	11	11	
	10	10	10	10	

Interpreting Your Personal Work Style Scores

Hero	Maverick	9-to-5er	Dissident
Easy to work with, supports the group and its objectives, helps other employees succeed, shows selfless behavior.	Idea person, thinks of new ways to do things, creative, always looking for a better way, decides quickly.	Always does his/her best on the job, comes to work on time and goes home on time. Doesn't make waves.	Frustrated, critical, finds fault with and places blame on others. Nothing is quite right, and it's always someone else's fault.

4

TRANSACTION ZONE THINKING IS SUPPORTED BY THE SHARED VALUES PROCESS®

Customer Centrix Model

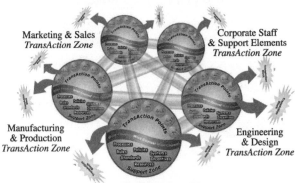

Marketing & Sales
TransAction Zone

Corporate Staff
& Support Elements
TransAction Zone

Manufacturing
& Production
TransAction Zone

Engineering
& Design
TransAction Zone

Information Technology (IT)
TransAction Zone

TransAction Zone Thinking & Behaviors

For twenty years, we've provided a methodology to over 200 organizations in Europe, Africa, India, China, North America, the Middle East, New Zealand and Australia. The Shared Values Process®/Operating System is based on eight universal values. The Process includes the *Values & Attitude Study*™, Shared Values Guidelines and Accountability-based behavior instruments. The heart of every *TransAction Zone*™ is the *TransAction Point*™. This Process delivers the solution for the five most important challenges facing all operations in creating *Great Customer TransActions*™:

The Five TransAction Zone Challenges™

The TransAction Point

1. The Process introduces **Ethical Standards.**

2. The Process challenges **Command & Control Thinking.**

3. The Process encourages **Leading by Example.**

4. The Process redefines the **Role of the Front-Line Worker.**

5. The Process creates an **Authentic Learning Environment.**

Lebow Company, Inc.
Corporate Headquarters: Bellevue, Washington, USA • Phone: (800) 423 - 9327, 001 425.828.3509
Email: contactus@lebowco.com • Web Site: www. lebowco.com

The Background of Shared Values® and the Values & Attitude Study™

In 1972, graduate students from the social psychology department of a major United States university began a research project to identify the link between job satisfaction and individual and organizational financial performance. They concluded that if a series of unique indices could be identified, this contribution to the study of performance improvement would be a major find.

Initially, 2.4 million workers and managers in the United States from 32 Standard Industrial Codes (SIC) were surveyed, but no conclusive correlations or links could be validated. So these graduate students broadened their search to an additional 40 countries in hope of uncovering such a relationship. The expansion generated an additional 14.6 million surveyed workers. In all, 17 million responses were reviewed. After almost three years of work and 17 million sources of data, no conclusive connection was validated between job satisfaction and individual or organizational performance. So, reluctantly, the students abandoned their work and viewed the data they had accumulated as having little or no value.

The Values & Attitude Study Was Created

The data gathered dust in a dark corner of the university's dead files for fifteen years until Rob Lebow and his research team started their own investigation. Their ultimate goal was to develop an instrument that organizations in any industry could use to uncover cultural challenges that impeded them from performing at exceptional performance levels. Additionally, they hoped to use this new instrument to predict future financial performance and merger opportunities and to uncover fraud in an operation. Today, the instrument is called the Values & Attitude Study™ (VAS), and it is on-line and available to organizations worldwide with a database of over 2,280 sites tested. Additionally, the GSA (General Services Administration of the United States

Government) has certified the instrument for use in any and all U.S. Federal Agencies.

The Lebow team identified three factors that the graduate students had not recognized. First, job satisfaction is not linked quantifiably to performance or morale. One person's happiness is personal to the extent of that individual's perceptions. Second, performance is the outcome of an organization's culture, or the context in which individuals work. And, third, job satisfaction or intrinsic motivators must be found deep in the human psyche.

Lebow postulated that obtaining job satisfaction was a spiritual idea and that ROI (return on investment) correlates could be obtained by looking at the comments generated by the 17 million voices waiting to be heard.

The turning point came when Lebow took a cue from John Naisbitt, author of the bestseller *Mega Trends*. In his book, Naisbitt used a most unorthodox approach to see the future, a future we now know Naisbitt predicted with uncanny accuracy. By totaling the column inches devoted in newspapers and magazines to the social, political, spiritual, and economic issues that would shape our future, Naisbitt postulated that those subjects that scored the highest would became the important issues of the future.

The approach Lebow took was to identify the most often addressed topics from the discarded surveys by country. And the surprise was that all the surveys from the different countries spoke of the same subjects. This became our 20th Century Rosetta Stone[1] that finally unlocked the secrets in the 17 million worldwide surveys that the original research had overlooked.

Buried in the literal comments, unnoticed by the young university researchers and their advisors, was a treasure trove of information that would unlock the key to high performance. The

---

[1] The Rosetta Stone, found in 1799, cracked the code that allowed Egyptologists to decipher Egyptian hieroglyphics.

answer that practically screamed at the Lebow research team was eye opening, to say the least. It was Values, not job satisfaction issues, that were at the heart of the matter; that were the link that opened the door between performance and what workers and managers sought. And Lebow's results suggested that there were eight values that mattered to all people throughout the world, regardless of nationality, race, religion, industry focus, gender, organizational status, or educational level.

Shared Values Were Identified

These eight values became the Shared Values that Lebow registered with the United States Patent Office in 1989, and which later became the basis for the early Shared Values Process®/Operating System and the TransAction Zone™ approach to creating Great Customer TransActions that are supported by the Shared Values Process®. Here is the unique list:

1. Treat others with uncompromising truth

2. Lavish trust on your associates

3. Mentor unselfishly

4. Be receptive to new ideas, regardless of their origin

5. Take personal risks for the organization's sake

6. Give credit where it's due

7. Do not touch dishonest dollars

8. Put the interests of others before your own

The Lebow research group concluded that these eight Shared Values—clearly important to people in all industries and all cultures worldwide—represent the major factors that contribute not only to job satisfaction and employee morale, but to an organization's performance, competitiveness, speed to change, innovation at every level, willingness to learn new things, and overall operational success. This was the universal Cultural ROI linking people to performance!

A Test Was Conducted

In 1989, the Lebow Company tested their hypothesis on a small chain of three-meal-a-day restaurants located along the Interstate 5 corridor in the Western United States. This small study showed a direct link between how well each of these restaurants delivered on these eight unique Shared Values and how each restaurant scored on bottom-line financial results. From this beginning in 1989, over 2,300 organizational sites (in which 50 or more employees were surveyed) have been studied. And in each case, the correlation between organizational performance and these universal Shared Values has been validated. Today, more than 305 organizations are using Shared Values principles in their daily efforts to achieve customer satisfaction and operational performance.

How the Values & Attitude Instrument Works

The key to understanding the link between performance and values is measuring the gap between the importance these eight Shared Values hold to the people within a particular organization and how well the organization delivers on the expectations of those staff members. From this gap (expectations versus organizational delivery on these eight values), a Values Tension Index™ (VTI™) for the organization is calculated and the Workplace Wellness Index™ is determined. The VAS, taken at regular intervals (every 14 to 16 months) helps an organization connect their *performance* to their *Cultural ROI* and predicts future opportunities and challenges. Today, the Values Tension Index™ is a leading indicator of an organization's *Future Operational Performance* and is used in the financial environment to uncover fraud during audits. Both the Sarbanes-Oxley Act 2002 and SAS-99 regulations (Statement of Auditing Standards) make the VAS a valuable companion to any financial audit in uncovering fraudulent practices. Additionally, the VAS is GSA approved, and the Lebow Company has been awarded its second five-year contract through 2009.

Training Components Include:

The Shared Values Process® is a 48-month cultural transformation process that moves an organization into a freedom-based culture and is comprised of five stages in twelve parts—with a heavy emphasis placed on a Train-the-Trainer approach. The basic vehicle for this transformation is the people within the organization. In Stage 1, the organization defines their TransAction Zone philosophy as they move away from control-based thinking. The Shared Values philosophy is introduced during Stage 2 of the Process. During Stage 3, the organization begins to redesign their systems to support TransAction Points and remove TransAction Blocks. In Stage 4, the organization designs their new Shared Values/TransAction Zone environment with a redesign that focuses on Customer Centrix™ behaviors. In Stage 5, business skills are improved.

The **Values & Attitude Study™** gives organizations insight into their level of competitiveness. The Study gives leaders operational benchmarks and best practices marks in 27 specific areas of their workplace and offers both international numbers and world-class scores. Included in the study are leadership levels, Shared Values levels, Intrinsic Motivation scores, and Staff Engagement scores that are interpreted into a Cultural ROI.

Workshops are a wonderful way to introduce and begin the Shared Values Journey. Workshops and follow-up sessions are offered in the following areas:

1. Introduction to Shared Values

2. Creating Great Customer TransActions Through Shared Values

3. Building TransAction Zone Skills in Senior Leaders

4. Moving from Supervisor to Wise Counsel—A Must for Managers and Supervisors

5. Ethics Training—The Shared Values Way

6. Diversity Training—Tools and Skills that Mean Something to Everyone and are Immediately Useful

7. The People Side to Sales Training—Not a Sales Process, but an Approach to "Keeping Customers for Life"

8. Team-Building Based on "Trust"—Not Fancy Techniques

9. Consensus Building for "Virtual Teams"

10. HR Systems—People Systems™ Development for the Eight Key Systems

11. Customer Centrix™ Environments Development and Design

Workshops, Keynotes & Speeches:

Rob Lebow is an accomplished master teacher, platform keynote speaker, author of the U.S. bestseller *A Journey Into The Heroic Environment*, and co-author of *Lasting Change* and *Accountability—Freedom and Responsibility Without Control.*

He is the founder and creator of the Shared Values Process®/Operating System and the new TransAction Zone™ redesign for organizations that want to create Great Customer TransActions™. The focus of his work for the past twenty years has been the implementation of the Shared Values Process as a method to establish a Freedom-Based Workplace. The outcome of this culture change for any size organization is the creation of a Great Customer TransAction by an operation's Front-Line Workers. It is the implementation of Shared Values that is the glue linking the Front-Line Worker to both the customer and the Wise Counsels of the organization (the old supervisory function no longer being necessary in such an environment). The Lebow Company's international operation was created to teach businesses in every industry around the world a revolutionary Process that promotes a change in the current belief that people need to be controlled, monitored, measured, and incentivized. Lebow believes in the Edwards Deming remark, *"Don't change the people or try to fix them...fix the systems."* And trust people to do great things.

The Lebow Company is celebrating its twentieth year in business. Rob has been married to his college sweetheart for the past thirty-six years, and they have a 20-year-old daughter. Corporate offices are in Bellevue, Washington, USA. He holds a master's degree in urban planning (MUP) from City University of New York and a bachelor's degree in international relations from Miami University, Oxford, Ohio. During his first twenty years in Corporate America, Rob held a senior marketing position at Microsoft Corporation, Redmond, Washington, and was a leading division manager at AVON Cosmetics of New York.

New Distributor & Associate Inquiries:

Worldwide distributor and associate opportunities are available to qualified independent consultants to large training organizations that want to install the Shared Values Process® or Heroic Environment®/Value-Based Operating System for existing or future clients. They should also be prepared to teach the Shared Values workshops and to administer the Values & Attitude Study™ plus additional behavior instruments.

Please contact us directly at:

The Lebow Company, Inc.
11820 Northup Way, Suite 101
Bellevue, WA 98005
United States of America

(800) 423-9327
001 (425) 828-3509
001 (425) 828-3552 (FAX)

Internet address: www.lebowco.com
Email address: Contactus@lebowco.com

INDEX

accountability/responsibility, 39, 73;
...and standards, 85

actual values. *See* values

American Society for Quality Control
(ASQC), 88

American Society of Training and
Development (ASTD), 5

autonomy: Give permission to act
with.... *See* Heroic Behavior, the five
Traits of...

Business Values/People Values, 41–49,
47, 48; dynamic equilibrium, 64
See also values

centralizing strategies, 140

chimpanzees: experiment, 27–29, 81. *See
also* Eight Principles of the
Heroic Environment

Coach, 72. *See* Wise Counsel–five roles
of...

'common sense', 163. *See also*
Entrepreneurial Intelligences,
the three

communications, 113

conditional thinking, 127–31; five
guidelines to overcome..., 129–30

control-based organizations: program
categories, 38–40

core values. *See* values

Counsel. *See* Wise Counsel–five roles of...

'Creative' element, 163. *See also*
Entrepreneurial Intelligences, the
three

credit. *See* Eight Principles of Heroic
Environment

customers: why companies lose...,
88–90, *88*

Deming, W. Edwards, 188.

dishonest dollars. *See* Eight Principles of
the Heroic Environment

Dissident, 96, 100–04. *See also* Dominant
Work Styles, the Four

Dominant Work Styles, the Four, 96,
120–22, 131, *96;* balance of the...,
122

Economist, The, 81–83, 150–51, *82*

Eight Principles of the Heroic:
Environment, 22–32, *22;* Dishonest
dollars, 30–31; Three Part Test, 31;
Giving Credit, 29–30; Lavish Trust,
23–24; Mentoring, 24–26, 79;
Receptivity to Ideas, 26; Risk-taking,
26–29; Chimpanzee experiment,
27–29; Self-interest, 31, 36;
Uncompromising Truth, 23

employees: 'fixing...', 37–38; treatment
of..., 78; wants, 76–79, *77*

Entrepreneurial Intelligences, the three,
163–168; balancing, 164–166;
common sense (practical), 163;
creativity (spiritual), 163; logical
(analytical), 163. *See also* Tracking
Motor, five elements

Everyday Values. *See* Sunday
Values/Everyday Values

Freud, Sigmund, 6

hangman, 59

Hero, 94–96. *See also* Dominant Work
Styles, the Four

Heroic Behavior(s), 4–6, 94; the eight...,
6; the Five Traits of..., 70–90

Heroic Environment, 6, 21–32, 63–64;
and the Navigator, 143–145; and
TransActions, 63–64; creating a..., 22;
Five Stages to the ..., 156–168. *See also*
Eight Principles of the Heroic
Environment

Hi-Touch/Hi-Power, 164–68

indifference, 89

information: filtered..., 140–41;
withholding..., 79

insider: make everyone feel like an...,
101. *See also* Heroic Behavior, five
traits of...

integrity: Act with.... *See* Heroic
Behavior, five traits of...

'internal advertising', 37

job satisfaction, 14, 16, 19

Journey into the Heroic Environment, A, 4

Keen Internal Vision, 46, 156

Lebow Company, 5

Logical Intelligence, 163. *See also*
   Entrepreneurial Intelligences, the
   three

Management: '...by Objective', 81–85;
   roles, 55, 141–43; tasks, 72. *See also*
   Pyramid(s)

Maverick, 96–98. *See also* Dominant
   Work Styles, the Four

Mentoring, 28–28. *See* Eight Principles
   of the Heroic Environment

mystery of organizational success, the, 120

Naisbitt, John, 183

Navigator(s), 137–38, 143–45, 149

"new citizenship", 143

9-to-5-er, 96, 98–100. *See also* Dominant
   Work Styles, the Four

No-Touch, 168

Nordstrom, 63, 74–75

Parker, Roger, 3,4

People Values. *See* Business
   Values/People Values

perceptual bias, 143

perfect job, 14, 15

Personal Heroics and the family, 6

Personal Work Style Assessment©, 5

Pyramid(s), 62, 65–66, *65:* ...and
   management, 141

Receptivity to new ideas. *See* Eight
   Principles of the Heroic Environment

Resource Connector. *See* Wise
   Counsel–five roles of...

responsibility. *See* accountability/
   responsibility

Risk-taking. *See* Eight Principles of
   Heroic Environment

Sarbanes-Oxley Act 2002, 5

Self-interests. *See* the Eight Principles of
   Heroic Environment

Shared Values, 4–6, 36–49; ...and
   controlbased organizations, 42; ...and
   the work environment, 16; ...in
   practice, 36–38. *See also* Values

Shared Values Process/Operating System
   (SVP®/OS), 5, 6

significant: Treat others as.... *See* Heroic
   Behavior, five traits of...

slogans, 37

standards, 38, 87

static observation, 151

Sunday Values/Everyday Values, 40–41.
   See also values

Terrorist, 104–105. *See also* Dominant
   Work Styles, Four

Toyota, 57–58

tracking motor, 150–51; five elements to
   keep it running, 156–68

TransAction(s); as a gift, 54; spelling, 60

TransActions Point(s), 54, 156

TransAction Steward. *See* Wise
   Counsel–five roles of...

TransAction Zone(s), 75–76, 156–57

truth: spinning the..., 43–44;
   uncompromising..., 23, 130. *See also*
   the Eight Principles of Heroic
   Environment

trust. *See* the Eight Principles of Heroic
   Environment

Trust others.... *See* Heroic Behavior, the
   five traits ...

upward coaching, 144

values: actual values, 65; as a filtering
   device, 43; core values, 41, 43;
   standards and..., 38; value-driven
   organization, 44. *See also* Business
   Values/People Values; Shared Values;
   Sunday Values/Everyday Values

Values & Attitude Study©, 5–6

values driven organization. *See* values

Visionary Leader. *See* Wise Counsel–five
   roles of...

Welch, Jack, 20

win-lose equation, 46

Wise Counsel, 73–75, 94, *56;* Five roles
   of ..., 55–57, *57;*

Work environment: ...and Shared
   Values, 15, 19; problems with..., 20

workplace, 3